WELCOME
COMMERCIAL MATCH FISHING HANDBOOK

Commercial match fishing is one of the fastest evolving areas of our sport. For years, anglers have dreamed of a 'professional circuit' - where they can win enough to sustain a living, and now, thanks to the evolution of commercial match fishing they are closer than ever to having one.

Fish 'O' Mania and Maver Match This each paid out top prizes of £50,000 last year; the Golden Reel winner collected £35,000 and the Fishing Association Supercup paid £30,000. Then there's the Parkdean Masters worth £15,000, with several more events paying £5k or more to the winner - and excitingly, new events are springing up all the time.

Anglers like Jamie Hughes, Andy Power and Andy Bennett have won enough over recent years to sustain a living, and with the likes of Kristian Jones, Jordan Holloway and an army of other young anglers nipping at their heels, it sometimes feels like angling already has its own pro tour.

Of course, the two biggest appeals about match fishing have always been its unpredictability and accessibility. Anyone can enter these events and stand a chance of winning. Get the tactics right, and even a newcomer to the sport can beat the best on a given day.

Consistently winning is something else altogether though. The standard of angling on our big events has never been higher, and the best get their rewards not through one stand out physical advantage or bait secret - but by several, hard earned tweaks that they apply to their fishing. Its these match winning edges that are the gold dust for the aspiring angler.

In this publication, my aim is to clearly illustrate the methods you need to win on commercial fisheries and explain the key principles that make them effective. Meanwhile, I will uncover as many of the match winning edges that I have learned over my last 20 years in angling journalism as I can.

For the beginner, this book should prove an invaluable guide to the tools you need to win, and for the more advanced angler a mine of useful tweaks and tips that you can build into your own fishing to gain an edge.

And a first piece of advice. While this guide will teach you a lot about the theory of winning commercial matches, there really is no substitute for getting out there and competing against the best. It's not always the most comfortable way to learn (no one likes a battering) but it is definitely the most effective.

In several chapters I've included short sections titled 'Influencers' these are the anglers that have really helped my understanding of particular methods and the winning mentality in particular. I'm indebted to each of them. Most of the sports top names are lovely people and will be only too happy to help you, you just need the confidence to approach them and ask any questions after the match has finished.

Good luck on your journey, may your elastic be stretched and your keepnets bulging.

Tom Scholey

BELOW:
Tom is a consistent top level match angler, and regular contributor to the angling press.

CONTENTS

COMMERCIAL MATCH FISHING HANDBOOK

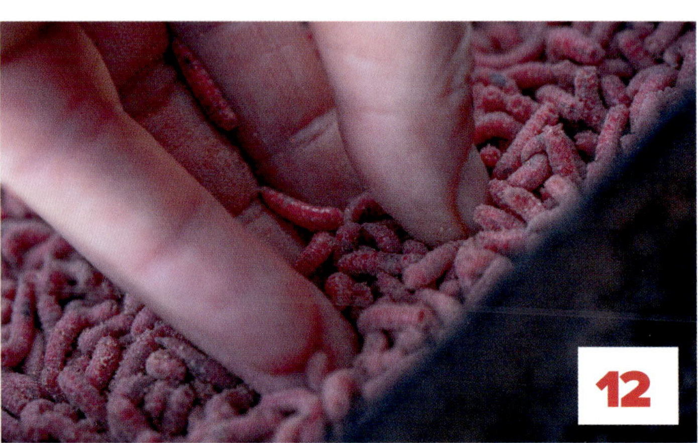

ISBN: 978 1 80282 715 6
Editor: Tom Scholey
Senior editor, specials: Roger Mortimer
Email: roger.mortimer@keypublishing.com
Cover design: Dan Jarman
Design: SJmagic DESIGN SERVICES, India
Advertising Sales Manager: Brodie Baxter
Email: brodie.baxter@keypublishing.com
Tel: 01780 755131
Advertising Production: Debi McGowan
Email: debi.mcgowan@keypublishing.com

SUBSCRIPTION/MAIL ORDER
Key Publishing Ltd, PO Box 300, Stamford, Lincs, PE9 1NA
Tel: 01780 480404
Subscriptions email: subs@keypublishing.com
Mail Order email: orders@keypublishing.com
Website: www.keypublishing.com/shop

PUBLISHING
Group CEO: Adrian Cox
Publisher, Books and Bookazines: Jonathan Jackson
Published by
Key Publishing Ltd, PO Box 100, Stamford, Lincs, PE9 1XQ
Tel: 01780 755131
Website: www.keypublishing.com

PRINTING
Precision Colour Printing Ltd, Haldane, Halesfield 1, Telford, Shropshire. TF7 4QQ

DISTRIBUTION
Seymour Distribution Ltd, 2 Poultry Avenue, London, EC1A 9PU
Enquiries Line: 02074 294000.

THE MODERN METHOD

The Method feeder, in all its guises, accounts for some tremendous match weights. The tactic has come a long way since it was first invented almost 40 years ago.

Over my lifetime in match fishing, the biggest single evolution in terms of techniques has been in the 'Method feeder'. As a young man I remember reading about the old 'Emstat' or 'coconut' feeders, which used to dominate at venues like Drayton Reservoir. Fast forward 20 or so years, and anglers such as Andy Findlay, Tommy Pickering and Nick Speed refined the Method feeder, to catch large numbers of F1s and skimmers - as well as the carp for which it was originally designed.

ABOVE:
This big F1 fell prey to a Method and wafter combo.

I have labelled this chapter the 'Modern Method' but I'm actually talking about a slightly broader church, covering hybrid feeder, and pellet feeder as well. The common theme is these are all bolt rigs, where you are effectively setting a 'carp trap' - a small pile of bait with a hookbait directly in or on it. When a carp sucks in this pile of bait, it hooks itself.

> **The softer action of the 'lesser modulus' rod is actually a distinct advantage when playing fish. It stops the hook from pulling and absorbs the lunges of the fish against the weight of the feeder.**

I've had a couple of very good teachers when it comes to this style of fishing. Firstly, the great Tommy Pickering - I've filmed with him a lot in recent years, and to watch him in action on this can only be described as poetry in motion. Secondly, Steve Ringer. Although I haven't spent much time on the bank with Steve, he has always been very open with me about how he approaches this style of fishing, and I've learned a lot from talking to him.

LEFT:
The Method feeder has evolved dramatically over the last 20 years.

cast short distances accurately than it is with longer rod (due to the smaller trajectory) and the fact that if the rod is shorter the fish pop up closer to you after the fight, meaning that you can net them more quickly.

When it comes to reel choice, I tend to use a 4000 size model with 8lb mainline (Daiwa Tournament or Guru Dragline are my favourites.) The main thing is to use something that is robust enough to stand up to the rigours of regular casting and winding in carp!

Method, Hybrid or Scoop?

I have played about with these different versions of the flatbed feeder and have concluded that a standard 'Method' is generally the best. There are two exceptions, I like a hybrid design when fishing at extreme distance, as I have confidence that the bait stays on better after the cast. And I sometimes like a pellet feeder for fishing up to cover, or islands, as the 'scoop-like' shape stops your bait from being wafted down the slope when there are a lot of fish feeding.

I use the Preston ICS Method, and pellet feeders, but favour the Guru Hybrid feeders for distance fishing. Again, this isn't a case of what is right and wrong, it's just what works for me.

On to rigs, and generally on commercial fisheries your feeders now have to be free running - so it is simply a case of tying a stop bead, to which your hooklength attaches, and having your feeder running free on the line above the bead.

When fishing at medium or long range for mixed fish, I will always use a fixed or semi fixed elasticated feeder as opposed to a free

I suppose my own style is a hybrid (no pun intended) of the approach of both men. As with all fishing, I've found an approach that works for me, and hopefully there will be a few pointers in here that you can learn from too.

Tackle for this kind of fishing has evolved massively over the last few years, with short rods being just one example of how we have refined feeder fishing kit to help us catch large numbers of fish quickly.

Obviously when it comes to fishing at range, big rods and reels are needed, but generally for most commercial fishing and casts of less than 40m, a ten foot rod is advantageous.

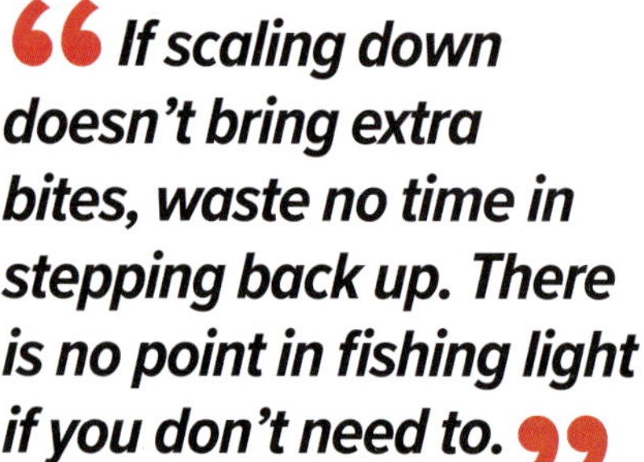

The good news for the more financially 'careful' anglers out there (and tight northerners like me) is that some of the best Method feeder rods are actually the cheapest. I remember watching Des Shipp win the £25,000 Parkdean Masters a couple of years ago, using a sub £100 rod from one of Preston Innovations' cheaper ranges.

The softer action of the 'lesser modulus' rod is actually a distinct advantage when playing fish. It stops the hook from pulling and absorbs the lunges of the fish against the weight of the feeder.

The two main advantages of short rods are that it is easier to

Powerline hooklengths, so if you are getting indications but not bites, never be afraid to scale down and see if it makes a difference. Obviously, have your drag set lightly though, so you make sure you land what you hook on this lighter tackle. And a final point on this - if scaling down doesn't bring extra bites, waste no time in stepping back up. There is no point in fishing light if you don't need to.

The Right Bait

When it comes to Method feeder fishing, bait prep is crucial. Your pellets need to be prepared so they are sticky enough to stay on the feeder for the cast but break down once in the water so they can be easily sucked in by passing fish. ▶

LEFT:
Daiwa's N'Zon rods are a great example of a budget beating range of rods that are perfect for mixed commercial Method work.

running one where its allowed. The elastic is helpful in cushioning the nods of any big fish. If elastic isn't allowed, Something else that can bring an advantage (again, where allowed) is to twizzle an eight inch length of line and have your feeder running on this. This offers extra protection and durability to the line above the feeder when the fish are in the net, and the resistance of the twizzled line stops the feeder bouncing about too much when you are playing fish, thus preventing hook pulls.

Onto the choice of hook, and it's basically two patterns for me. In my eyes a Guru QM1 is simply the best carp feeder hook ever made. I use these in a size 10 or size 12 generally, when big carp are the target. Their circular shape means they have excellent hold - when one goes in, they rarely come out. When mixed fish are the target, and I'm expecting more F1s and skimmers, I do like a smaller size and pattern though. For this, it's a size 16 Guru SLWG.

My rule of thumb is to fish fairly positive hooklengths when Method feeder fishing, as you often encounter BIG fish, and when this happens, you want to land them. 0.17mm diameter Reflo Power is the usual choice - but I will step up to 0.19mm or even 0.21mm if there are some real units on the cards.

The above said, on pressured venues where you are targeting a mixture of F1s and carp, sometimes fishing lighter hooklengths is an advantage. I have caught a lot of fish in the past using 0.13mm

LEFT:
A Method Mould means you can load your feeder perfectly every time

BELOW:
Robust reel line, and a workhorse of a reel is important for a summer Method session.

I can give a rough guide on how to do this - but be mindful that every batch of pellets is different, so it's important you find a formula that works for you.

There are two types of micro pellet commonly available, named here after the companies that make them. First up, Coppins pellets. To prepare these for the feeder, I soak them for around ten minutes in water, then drain them and put them in a plastic bag with the air taken out of it. These are then left in the fridge overnight, to give them chance to properly absorb the water.

Next up, the slightly more common Skrettings pellets. These are darker in colour and require less preparation time. I will happily prepare these on the bank before fishing. All I do is soak them in water for around two minutes, then drain and leave to stand for around 40 minutes before use.

The ideal is a pellet with a soft outer but 'firmish' core, which binds easily when you squeeze it on to the feeder. Remember, you can always test how your pellets work by dropping a loaded feeder in a bait box full of water. Ideally, pellets should begin coming off the feeder within a minute of it entering the water.

In terms of hook baits, there are lots of options out there. I will go into more details on this in the winter Method chapter at the end of the publication, but for most

summer work I have three go-to baits. The first is a Fjuka Wafter in pink, natural or yellow. The second is a hard 6mm pellet, and the third is a single red maggot. With the exception of maggots, which I hook very thinly, I always like to band, spike or hair rig my hookbait, so I have the maximum amount of hook exposed.

Generally, in the warmer months I will fish a Method feeder within catapult range, so I can loosefeed some hard pellets over the top while I am fishing. This can often

> ## 66 *My rule of thumb is to fish fairly positive hooklengths when Method feeder fishing, as you often encounter BIG fish.* 99

pull in extra fish, as well as giving you the chance to alternate other methods - such as a bomb or a waggler over the same line.

Accuracy?

There's a great deal written or broadcast about casting accuracy in angling but where the Method is concerned it isn't *necessarily* vital. It depends how and where you are fishing it. If it's about casting tight to the margins of islands, or to a particular area of shallow water, it's important. However, if you're fishing in open water of a consistent depth, not so much. One of the benefits of the Method is that it is effectively a self-feeding 'trap' so wherever you throw it, it is working for you. That said, there is often some wisdom in casting in a relatively tight area in

ABOVE LEFT:
Guru QM1 Hooks are my choice when big carp are the target, and I hair rig wherever possible.

ABOVE RIGHT:
Summer hookbait choice is kept very simple. Wafters, pellets, or maggots.

BELOW:
A through or mid action rod is best on the Method feeder to absorb the lunges of any fish hooked.

summer if the fish are feeding so you can generate an element of competition.

Keep it Slack!

One thing I would caution against when Method fishing is having too tight a line between your tip and your feeder. Not only does this increase the chance of you committing Tom Pickering's cardinal sin of moving the feeder while it's set, but I also think that the fact you have tight line running through the water means you are more prone to spook fish. I fish the lightest tip I can get away with (generally about 1oz) and fish with a very small amount of tension in the rod. This means that if a fish should brush into the line, it isn't going to move the feeder.

Another key point, which only experience can really teach you, is that you have to sit on your hands with this kind of fishing. Often, you will have a lot of fish in your peg, and your tip might be doing a merry old dance - but make sure you are as certain as you can be that the fish is on before you pick the rod up. It's all well and good striking at thin air, but it doesn't weigh very much!

As you can no doubt tell, Method feeder is one of the simplest techniques out there - but pay attention to the small details, and you can easily gain an advantage. One tiny tweak that has caught me loads of extra fish has been changing the length of my hooklength. I used to just use four inch hooklengths, but on those

INFLUENCER...

Tom Pickering has helped so much with my understanding of this style. His knowledge of how feeders work underwater, twinned with a world-class angling brain has seen him develop the Method into a match winner. When you speak to him about the development of the Method, he is also keen to credit Andy Findlay - who he spoke to endlessly when the two men worked together at Preston Innovations.

> **" The Method feeder is one of the simplest techniques out there - but pay attention to the small details, and you can easily gain an advantage. "**

cagey days when the fish don't quite want to feed confidently, using a five or even a six inch hooklength can bring an advantage.

If you are a regular Method angler, hopefully there are a few pointers in here to help you improve your technique. If you aren't- I would urge you to get out and work on this, as on its day, it's one of the simplest ways to win matches. ■

LEFT:
Heavy line and a robust hook are my default choice. I only go light if I really need to.

THE BANKER METHOD

For one method to get a bite on the toughest day or add that final fish for a late match win. It has to be maggots.

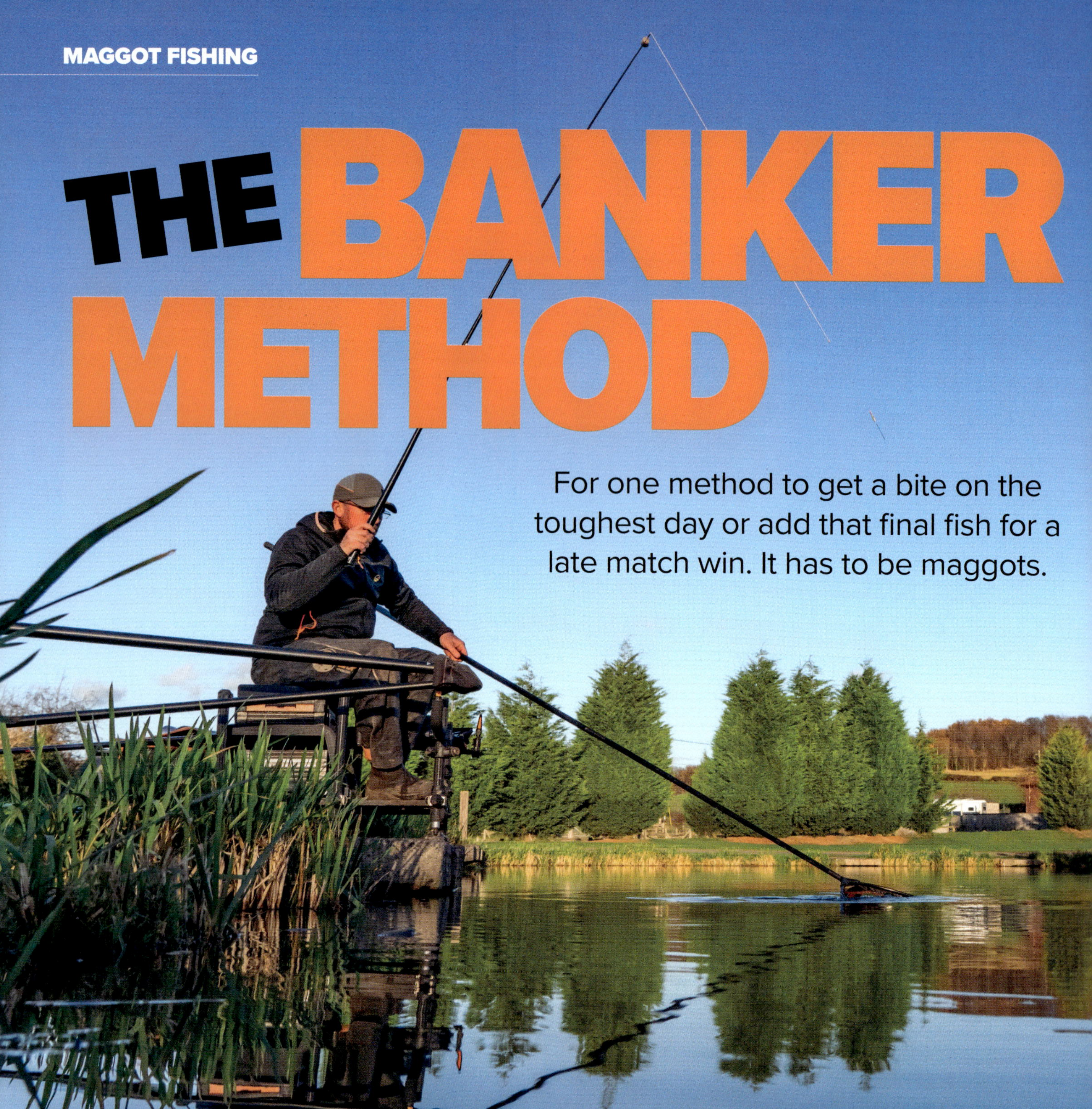

ABOVE: Spring, Autumn or Winter, maggots are one of the best ways of building a peg. Andy Bennett (pictured) has taken commercial maggot fishing to the next level over recent years.

For the eight coolest months of the year, maggots form a staple part of my commercial fisheries attack. The first big edge that they have over other baits is that every species of fish will eat them. One theme you will note throughout this book is the need to create competition in your peg. Achieve this, and the fish become so much easier to catch. Because all species of fish eat maggots, they are one of the very best baits for generating this competition.

Of course, every venue and every peg demands its own approach but generally speaking I like to locate a maggot line where I can comfortably throw bait - so anywhere between a top four and a top six (4m-6m) from the bank. Often, a maggot swim is best left a while before you fish it, so by locating it close in an area that's easy to feed by hand, you can build it effortlessly while fishing elsewhere.

Another key consideration is the make-up of the lake bed. It is well worth spending some time with a plummet looking for a silt free area to fish over. Hold your plummet a couple of feet off the bottom, then let it drop on a slack line. If it sticks in the bottom, you know you are on silt. Ideally, you should find a hard area where you know your bait can sit on the bottom without sinking in to the silt, generally the closer you come to the near shelf, the firmer the bottom will be.

I will discuss later how close to yourself you should look to fish and why - but as a general rule, in the first instance locate your swim where you are confident the fish will come to compete. The colder, and clearer the water the further away this will be. You can always bring the fish closer later if the session is going well.

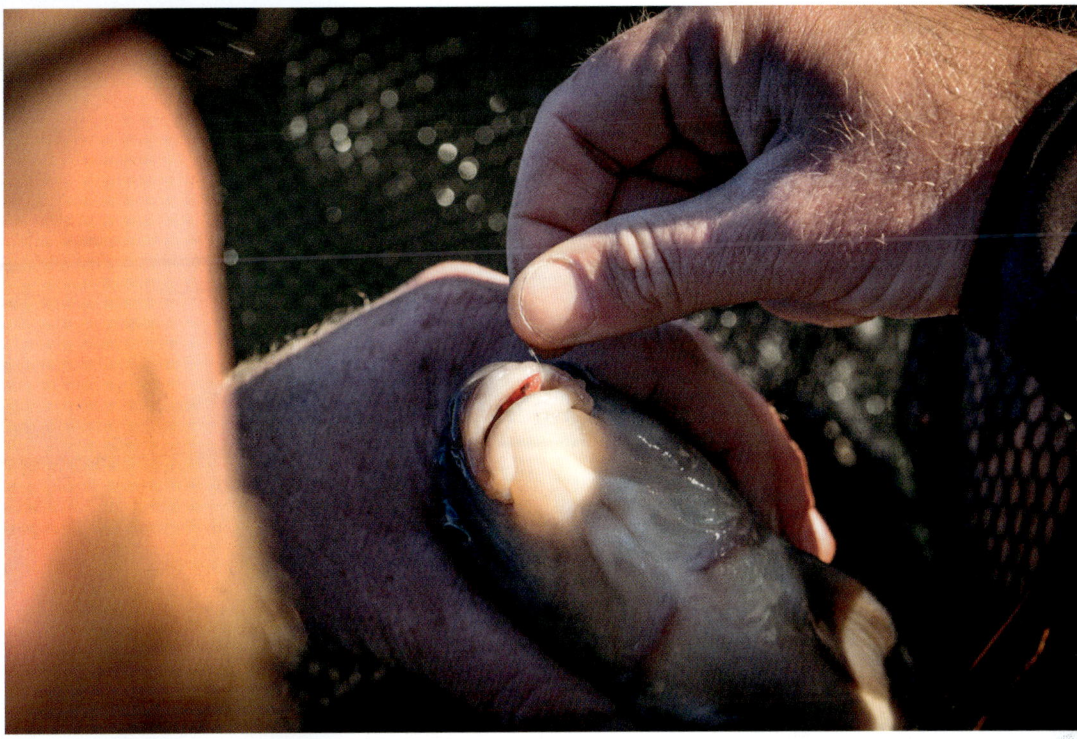

ABOVE:
Perfect! You know you have your rigs and feeding right when wary F1s like this are hooked in the lip.

Tackle

A maggot swim will help you catch everything that swims - at least until the carp and F1s move in and push the other fish out. For this reason, balance is critical. You want a set up that allows you to catch a three ounce roach one put in but strong enough to land a 4lb F1 on your next.

Soft, hollow or hybrid elastic is great here, when used in conjunction with a puller bung, or puller kit. The beauty of this setup is that it gives you a lovely soft elastic, with the capability to puller some out at the netting stage and gain control of the fish. Importantly, this elastic should be set fairly soft, so plenty comes out on the strike, and the hooked fish can swim out of your peg without disturbing anything else that might be feeding in the area. Generally, I look for something around a 6-8 grade elastic for mixed work, but may go lighter if I was expecting predominantly silverfish, or heavier if I was expecting just F1s and carp.

I fish a robust mainline, generally 0.15mm diameter or stronger. If things go to plan, you can end up really bagging on maggots in the later stages of the day, so you need a set up that is resilient enough to help you put a big weight together quickly. Also, because my presentation often centres around fishing maggots on the drop, a thicker mainline falls nice and ▶

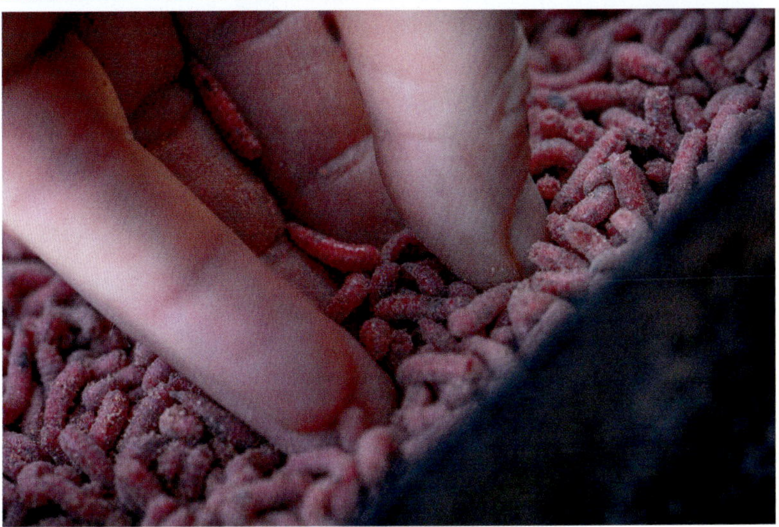

LEFT:
Red maggots are my choice for carp and F1s. Mixed red and whites can work well when mixed silvers and F1s are the target.

slowly through the water, giving a very natural fall.

There are three main shooting patterns that come in to play for me. The first is a tapered bulk, so No10 or No11 droppers starting six inches apart next to the hooklength loop, and getting progressively closer, finishing anywhere between a third and halfway up the rig. This is for catching fish on the drop, and on harder days is often my go-to choice.

The next is a bulk and droppers. For this, I have two No10 droppers six inches apart, then a bulk of No10s six inches above this. This can be great when mixed fish are present, including some better F1s and carp lower in the water column, as it gets the bait down to where the bigger fish

> **66 This elastic should be set fairly soft, so plenty comes out on the strike, and the hooked fish can swim out of your peg without disturbing anything else. 99**

are quickly, but still affords nice presentation in the crucial last couple of feet of water.

Finally, I have my bagging rig. This is just a bulk of shot at the top of the hooklength knot. This one comes to the fore when there are lots of feeding carp and F1s present - generally in the later part of the session. The beauty of this is it gives really positive presentation, keeping line bites to a minimum, and resulting in really positive bites.

Float choice is a slim, carbon stemmed pattern with a visible hollow bristle that I can dot down. I always use back shot when maggot fishing, to help me keep control of the rig, and temper the fall when fishing on the drop. On tougher days, there can

ABOVE LEFT:
Slim floats that follow the bait through the water are best for maggots. Note the visible, hollow bristle.

ABOVE RIGHT:
A well-stocked hook box is a maggot angler's best friend. Experimenting with different length hooklengths will often help you get more bites.

LEFT: Where stocked, ide are so often the first to the maggot party. Often, you enjoy a good run of them before they disappear - and bigger carp and F1s take their place.

be an advantage in using very light floats with the strung pattern, to really help you achieve the most natural presentation possible, but generally a 4x12 or 4x14 float in three to 6ft of water is about right.

Hooks

There are two patterns I favour for this kind or work. On harder days, I like a light pattern like a Gamakatsu Green (size 16 - no smaller) or a Guru F1 Maggot in an 18 or a 20. These super light patterns give great presentation, and on tough days using them as opposed to thicker wire patterns can be the difference between a fish a chuck, and not getting a bite.

The other pattern that I favour is a rounder bend, like a Guru F1 Pellet in a size 18 or 20, or on really prolific days, a Guru SLWG. When the fishing is good, these offer a heavier alternative so you can play the fish with a bit more aggression and build a weight quickly. These thicker patterns also suit fishing double maggot which can be deadly for sorting out the bigger fish at times.

One final point on rigs is hooklength length. This is worth particular consideration when maggot fishing. If I am looking to catch on the drop with the

▶

ABOVE:
Light, balanced tackle is essential for maggots, soft enough to land small fish, but with enough grunt to tackle carp and F1s.

LEFT:
Feeding little and often is normally the best way to get a swim going.

LEFT:
Big F1s like this are suckers for a well presented maggot.

A shorter hooklength can be a real advantage at times, as it shows up bites more quickly, and helps you nail those shy biting F1s.

ABOVE:
If you have trouble with missed bites, liners and foul hookers, don't be afraid to bring the fish closer.

RIGHT:
Lightly nick the maggot on the hook for the most natural presentation. The hook here is a size 18 Guru F1 maggot.

light, strung rig, a six inch or eight inch hooklength is perfect, as it encourages a natural fall, and gives the fish chance to get the bait in its mouth before they feel any resistance. In contrast, when fishing more on the bottom with bulk and dropper rig, or the bulk rig, a shorter hooklength can be a real advantage at times, as it shows up bites more quickly, and helps you nail those shy biting F1s.

Feeding

As I've said, a maggot line is often best built up through the day, so a little and often feeding approach can be a good way to prime a maggot swim. I tend to start by feeding a dozen or so maggots every five minutes and like to leave the line for at least a couple of hours before I have a look on it. This is generally enough time for me to build up a volume of fish in the peg and get them competing.

The real strength of maggots as a bait, is that you can then adapt your feeding to change your peg if you need to. Obviously, if you drop in and bigger fish are present, maintaining the little and often pattern is the right thing to do. But if your drop in and fish of the wrong stamp are there, it can be well worth either upping the ante with the loose feeding, or picking up the big pot to force the fish that are present down to the bottom, thus intensifying the competition and drawing in bigger fish.

One common problem that can be encountered with maggots is too many fish, feeding at all levels in the water column. This may sound a nice problem to have, but it can be a nightmare - with foul hooked fish and line bites often the result.

I touched on one possible solution earlier, and that is to feed closer to the bank towards you.

This is a deadly trick, as the fish rarely want to be high in the water near bankside disturbance (you), plus the bottom is often firmer here too, leading to cleaner bites. When the fish are feeding well, never be afraid to take a section off, and make the fish come to you. You can

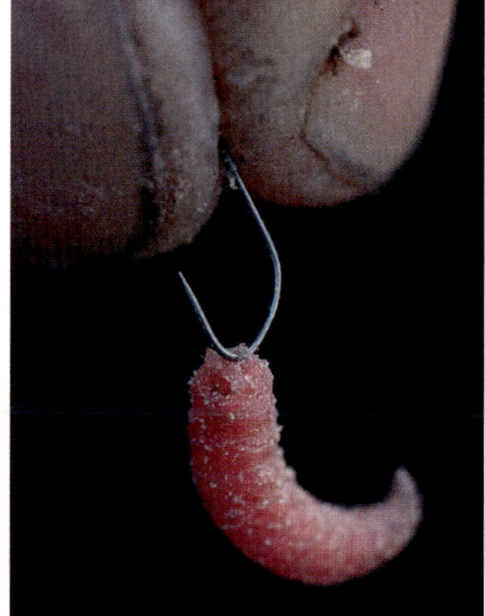

LEFT:
A maggot caught mixed net for Kristian Jones. This is the real strength of the bait, you can catch both silvers, and F1s and carp ensuring you are feeding your net throughout the session.

often be a lot more effective at very close range.

A final point on maggots. I think feeding a line with a bait like maggots, that attracts all species of fish can often have a positive effect on your whole swim. Even if you don't end up catching on maggots, I think the fact that you have had them dropping through the water will have pulled fish into your area.

As a part of a bigger plan for a match, where other lines are employed they are invaluable, giving you somewhere to go for a few bites, even if it is from silvers, while other lines are rested. They help you build your peg and feed your net throughout the session. ■

KEY POINTS ON MAGGOTS

- Fish a light balanced set-up to catch everything that swims.
- Feed little and often to generate competition.
- Look to catch through the water if it's hard, but bulked down rigs score well when the fish turn up.
- Problems with line bites or foul hookers? Bring the fish towards you, where you can nail them to the bottom.

> **When the fish are feeding well, never be afraid to take a section off, and make the fish come to you. You can often be a lot more effective at very close range.**

MASTER THE MUDLINE

In warm weather, carp and F1s love to feed in shallow water, and there's no better place to target than the mudline.

ABOVE:
Many commercials are now purpose built to give anglers a 'mud line' to fish up to.

Carp and F1s love feeding in shallow water during the summer months. Their competitive nature forces fish up into shallows, often seeing them feed comfortably in just 12in of water or less. Welcome to the mudline!

The 'mudline' as many match anglers call it, is simply the area of shallow water found tight against the near and far margins of commercial lakes, often featuring a bare bank, hence the term mudline. While some venues are well pruned, clear of any overhanging vegetation, some might require a bit of pruning to achieve perfect presentation. It is also worth remembering that not all venues have shallow water tight against the bank, thanks to years of erosion. These places require a different approach.

Choose the Correct Depth

The beauty of the mudline is, because you have bare bank, you can often get into pretty much whatever depth you want. Fishing in the right depth couldn't be more important. Fish too deep and you'll be plagued with liners and foul hookers, but fish in too shallow water and the fish will either not come in at all or lack confidence when they do.

When choosing your depth, you need to consider the fish you're looking to catch. If you're targeting a mix of small carp and F1s, 12-16 inches will be about right. Yet when fishing venues with a stocking of larger carp I'd be more confident fishing in slightly deeper water to give those wiser fish more confidence to feed.

On certain days during the height of summer, big carp will often venture into super shallow depths, happy to almost beach themselves in search of food. On some occasions you'll get bites in less than eight inches of water and empty it, so it can be worth a try. Be

RIGHT:
Micros are a staple bait in deeper swims, or when groundbait sends the fish crazy.

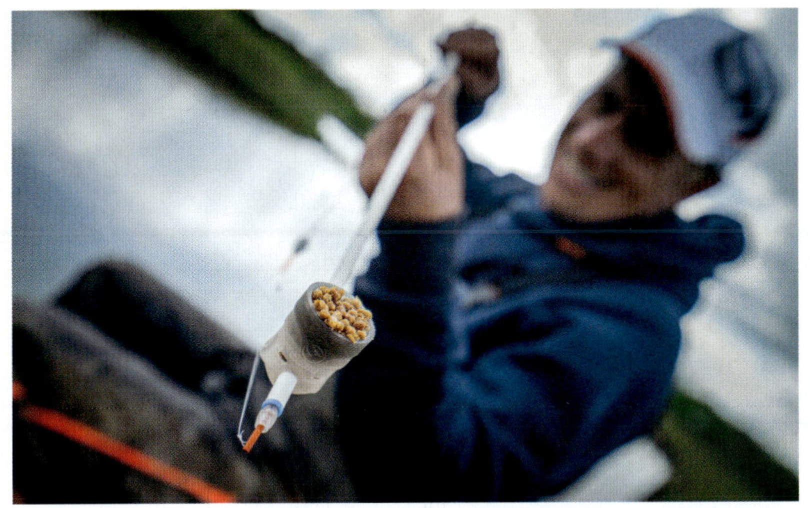

careful not to be left chasing your own tail trying to catch fish that simply can't be caught though. If you are struggling to hook the fish that you can see, drop down into slightly deeper water and you'll probably find you can catch them.

Fishing as tight as you can against the bank is arguably the most important part of mudline fishing. This is crucial to prevent feeding fish from getting behind your rig and causing you a major headache with liners and foul hookers.

> ***"Fishing as tight as you can against the bank is arguably the most important part of mudline fishing."***

On certain venues like Partridge Lakes Fishery, most pegs have purpose-built mud holes, both across and down the edges. These often resemble a cut, or slight V shape in the bank. When tackling pegs like this, I like to fish in a corner of the mudline, offering me an angle of protection from feeding fish, yet again preventing them from getting behind my float. Blocking off an entrance to hungry fish might sound slightly backwards but this can really work in your favour. When fishing in the mud, carp and F1s often rush into the feed from all angles, resulting in missed bites. If you limit the way fish can enter your swim, this straightaway slows everything down and results in more bites converting into landed fish. If you can find your desired depth, tight to the bank, you're onto a winner.

It is worth remembering that every day is different with the conditions often dictating the depth of water which the fish are happy to feed in. On bright, flat calm days for example it can be beneficial to drop down the slope into slightly deeper water. Yes, this does contradict ▶

LEFT:
Make sure your pole pot is as close to the end of your pole as possible for ultimate accuracy.

BELOW:
Marking the depth on your top kit gives a quick reference, often a good depth one day will also work well again the next.

BOTTOM:
Feeding every put in is essential, as disturbance from hooked fish will spread your bait everywhere.

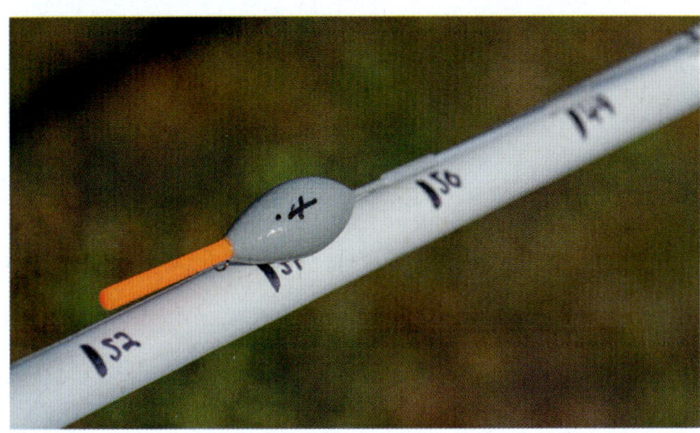

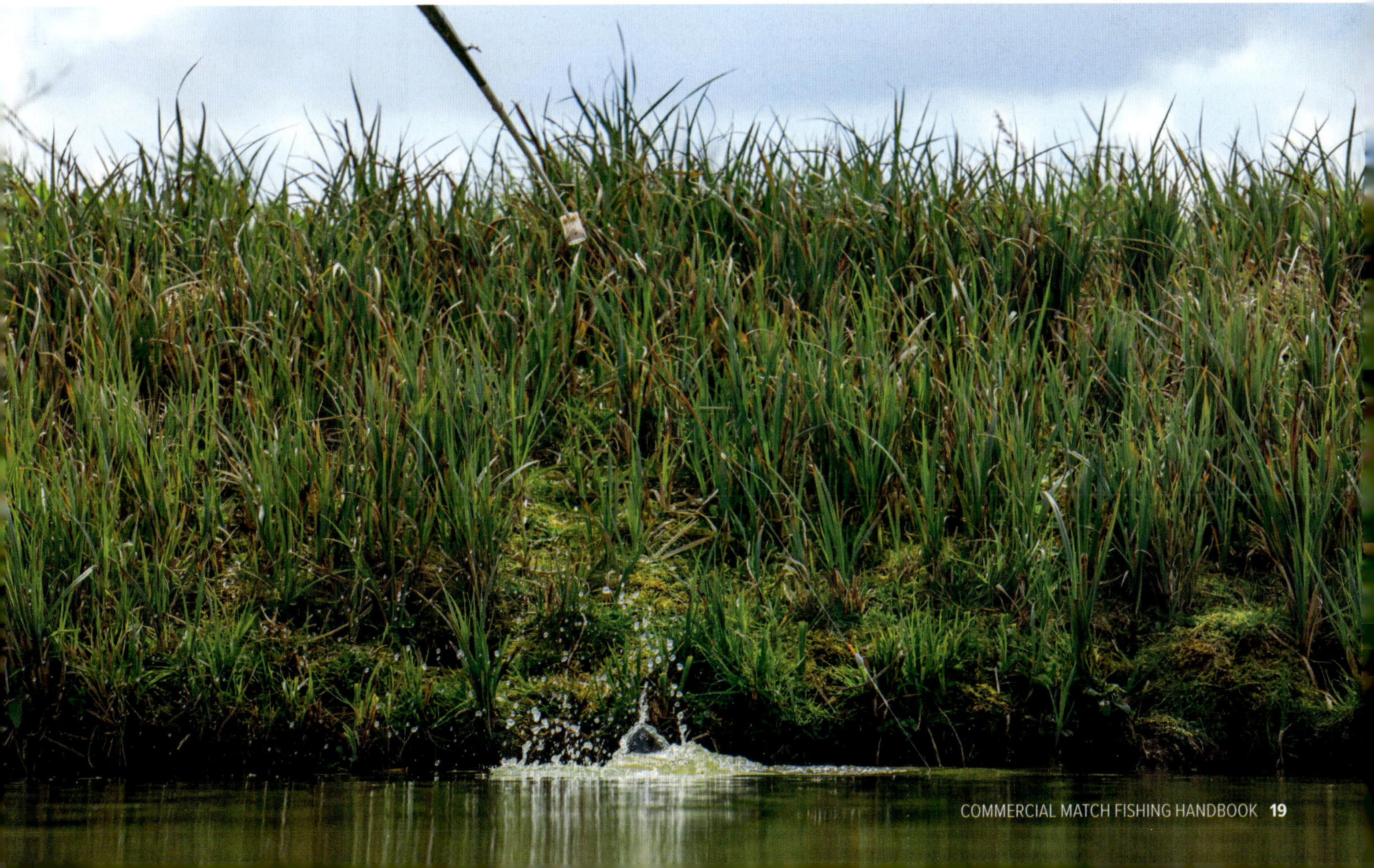

my earlier thoughts on fishing tight against the far bank, but if the fish aren't willing to feed in the depth found there, you're simply wasting your time. This can alter throughout the day, so stay vigilant and don't be afraid to change.

Your Plummet Matters

When plumbing up on slopes, it's important that you use a heavy plummet so you can really read the bottom. I opt for a 30g version enabling me to easily read the depth at distance. Where the bottom is flat or slightly sloping, I tend to fish around an inch over depth. This is just enough to ensure my hook bait is sat still on the bottom. Where the bottom is uneven and slopes away quickly, I'll often fish at least two inches over depth to ensure my hook bait is still on the bottom if my rig drifts slightly out of position.

Now that we have established where you need to fish, I'll to run through my rig of choice. Starting with my mainline. This has to be 0.19mm, a diameter that lets you land everything you hook, plus if you're looking to save time in the preparation department, you can use the same rig multiple times without giving it a second thought.

LEFT:
The mudline is a great way of targeting F1s, which will often feed all day if you find the right depth to target them in.

BELOW:
Get your feeding right, and you will soon put a big weight together.

> **I'm a huge fan of back shots. In the context of mudlines specifically, I like to use two No8 shots around three inches above my float.**

A thicker mainline also eliminates tangles, helping you stay efficient when the fishing gets going.

When it comes to hooklength choice, I like to scale down slightly to 0.13mm or 0.15mm, depending on how prolific the fishing is and the species I'm catching. If the fishing is fast and furious, I'll happily choose a 0.15mm hooklength to prevent any breakages caused by wear on my landing net head. If some larger carp are in on the action this would also warrant a stronger hooklength, giving me more confidence when playing them in match conditions.

When fishing in 13in or less I'll opt for a 2in hooklength, and from 14in upwards a 3in hooklength would always be my choice. This allows me to position my bulk of shot in proportion to the depth of my rig, keeping it nailed where I want it. Small edges like this really do make a big difference.

In terms of shotting, a bulk of No8 shot right above my hooklength knot is the only way for me. In such shallow water there really is no place for strung out shot. You're trying to achieve perfectly still presentation and this bulk gives you just that. A bulk in this

LEFT:
Big carp like this often move in on the mudline late in the session.

BELOW:
A variety of hook baits, plus groundbait and micros are needed for a day on the mudline.

BOTTOM:
Setting up your seatbox so you can fish comfortably is vital when targeting the mudline.

place also exaggerates your bites massively, most of the time pulling the entire float bristle under at a million miles per hour as the fish sucks in your hook bait. Float choice is massive too. I always opt for a 0.4g RW Muddie float, a pattern designed specifically for mudline fishing. Whatever float you choose it's important that it's short, has a round body for stability, a glass or carbon stem for strength and a thick 2mm hollow bristle for visibility and buoyancy. A float with a thin bristle would be far too sensitive, and likely submerge as a nearby fish wafts its tail.

Onto the business end. My hook choice when fishing the mudline is a size 16 Super LWG, a hook that never lets me down. They're ▶

ultra-sharp and strong enough to land just about anything you're likely to hook. If some bigger carp are making an appearance, I'll happily step up to a size 14.

Elastic Choice

Choosing the correct elastic becomes super important when fishing in such shallow water. I always opt for a soft-to-medium hollow elastic, a white Hydro from Daiwa or 10 hollow from Preston Innovations are great examples. The less commotion you cause when hooking into an unsuspecting fish the better. A light elastic allows them to glide out of your swim without completely scattering the remaining feeding shoal. A heavy elastic would cause your hooked fish to splash excessively on the surface and this is likely to be detrimental.

Throughout this publication you'll notice that I'm a huge fan of back shots. In the context of mudlines specifically, I like to use two No8 shots around three inches above my float. This anchors my pole float super accurately over my feed while waiting for a bite. When fish venture into such shallow depths their size causes lots of water movement which can result in your float drifting away from your neatly presented pile of bait. By using back shot, I'm minimising this movement, always nailing my hookbait directly over my loose fed groundbait or pellets. Ultimately, the longer you can keep your bait in position, the more fish you'll catch.

Lash Length

My final comment in the rig department must be on lash length – the distance between pole tip and float, or more accurately, pole tip and back shot. The most common mistake I see here is having a lash that is way too short. Unless you're absolutely bagging, and the fish have thrown caution to the wind, you get more bites with a longer lash simply because you spook less fish. Especially when fishing in such shallow depths, fish that are approaching with caution can be spooked by a pole tip too low to the water, particularly on bright sunny days. There are of course exceptions, for example when fishing at close range down the edge, you can hold your pole tight against the banking, helping you keep it

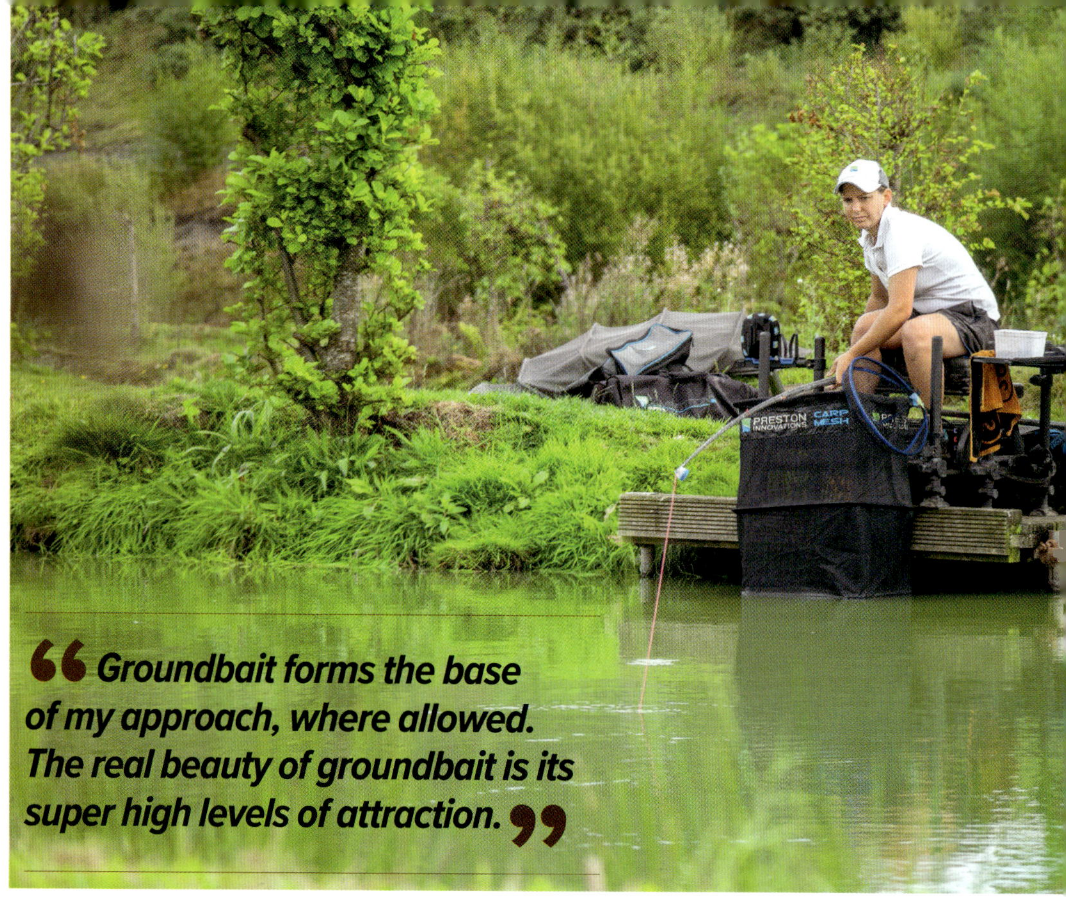

> **Groundbait forms the base of my approach, where allowed. The real beauty of groundbait is its super high levels of attraction.**

completely still, eliminating any spooking of feeding fish. Around 18in is great when fishing at distance, although I'll shorten this slightly to 12in when fishing in the edge.

Mudline Bait Choice

Generally, my hookbait choice will be three maggots, a piece of corn, a 4mm expander, a cube of meat or half a worm. Whatever you choose, it's important to have a range to pick from. I'll always keep at least three in my armoury giving me the chance to change throughout the day.

In terms of feed baits, groundbait and micro pellets are always my go-to. Groundbait forms the base of my approach, where allowed. The real beauty of groundbait is its super high levels of attraction. This pull is a must when trying to drag fish into such shallow water. It produces a visual cloud of attraction, with the coloured water often leading to the fish feeding with increased confidence. When mixing your groundbait it's important that you add plenty of water, so you get a nice damp mix, that when potted in loose will hug the bottom.

As the session progresses, I might need to rope in my second bait of choice, the micro pellet. This is often necessary when I have too many fish feeding in my swim, causing missed bites and foul hooked fish. Micros add food content to my mix but reduce its level of attraction. By feeding a mixture of micros and groundbait, fewer fish will come

in to investigate at any one time. If my swim begins to slow, I'll add more groundbait to my mix. A 'working' bait tub is crucial to allow me to adjust this throughout the day. I'll often have three bait tubs in operation. One loaded with just groundbait, another full of micro pellets and a third 'working' tub containing some percentage of micros and groundbait, that I alter to suit how the swim is developing.

Some occasions might see me introduce micro pellets on their own. A good example of this would be if my peg was full of newly stocked fish. In this instance any groundbait could send them into a feeding frenzy causing chaos in the peg.

Pay attention to how you set your pole rollers up, so you can bring the fish back with minimum disturbance.

BELOW:
Guru SLWG hooks are a brilliant choice on the mudline, as they combine strength and finesse.

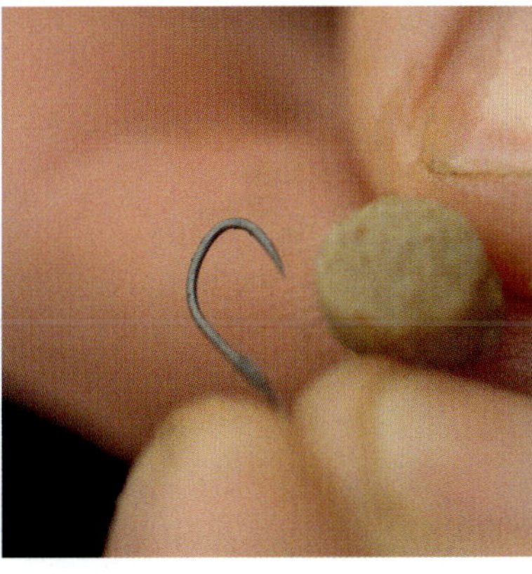

LEFT:
When the going is tough, a 4mm expander is one of the best hook baits going.

RIGHT:
The RW Muddie is my go-to pattern for mudline work, but there are lots of similar patterns available.

Another situation might be if I couldn't find shallow enough water. If you're faced with a mudline over 18 inches deep, I'd be wary of introducing any groundbait at all. Groundbait in that depth is likely to cause fish to venture off the bottom, yet again resulting in missed bites and foul hooked fish.

Go Potty

Now that I have discussed the bait in question, let's talk pots. The medium and large Guru pole pots are my pots of choice when fishing the mudline. As a rule, I'll start on my large pot allowing me to feed enough bait to quickly draw in a feeding fish. As my swim builds, I'll drop down to a medium pole pot to reduce the volume of bait entering my swim. With less bait in my peg, I'd expect quicker bites. To get the most from mudline fishing it's important to stay busy, swapping pots as your swim changes throughout the day.

If there's one thing you must nail, when it comes to mudline fishing, it's your regularity of feeding. After a distinct splash or sign of a fish disturbing your peg it's crucial that you ship back and refill your pole pot. You can then reset your 'trap' in wait of a feeding fish. With few exceptions, I'll feed a pole pot of bait every time I ship out to the mudline. When you get to your desired position, take some care to gently dip your pole pot under the water, allowing gravity to pull

your bait out of the pot in a linear fashion to the bottom. By tapping your bait out from a height to splash you'll create an unnecessarily large spread, making it much harder to get a bite. The sound of your bait landing will also cause fish to rush into your swim often resulting in missed bites.

On most occasions I'll start my session with one large Guru pole pot, not the cupping kit. There's simply no need. With the fish you're hoping to catch often just metres away, a small amount of bait is all that's needed to nail your first. As my day progresses, I may want to rest my mudline. On this occasion I'll employ my cupping kit to pot around 100ml of groundbait on my swim before resting the line. This should create enough attraction to reset my peg and generate another run of bites. Although I would never start in this way, on some occasions

a much greater volume of bait might be required to bring in feeding fish. A barrage of groundbait fed via your large cupping kit can be the way if you see little sign of an arrival - and want to gamble for a run of fish.

The ideal scenario though is controlled feeding, to keep the fish competing - so they eat your hookbait in the fastest possible time. ■

RIGHT:
A variety of different size pots is useful so you can regulate the amount you feed easily.

BELOW:
Note the shot bulked together at the top of the hooklength.

MEAT MANIA

Where it's allowed, meat can be a devastating bait during the warmer months, as the fish look to stock up on protein. Here is how to get the best from it.

Whether you love or loath it, there's simply no denying the effectiveness of meat. For me, it's right up there with maggots, worms and paste in the 'super bait' category. When fish switch on to it, they often do so with gay abandon - and you are winning. It's easy to see why - with such a high protein content, carp and F1s in most commercials struggle to resist it when they need to stock up on nutrients.

Unfortunately, due to its potential danger to water quality when fed in extreme quantities, some fisheries have banned the use of meat in all its forms. If you do plan to use it, always check with the fishery beforehand.

Be Ready in Spring

When it comes to fishing with meat, timing is everything. There are times when the bait is unbeatable - and also times when it's best left at home. With water temperatures on the higher side, spring, summer, and autumn are often the best seasons to employ a meat approach. Being so rich in protein, carp and F1s will only eat meat in any volume when they're active and competing for food. Spring is a particularly exciting time to bring meat into your attack, with fish actively looking to feed on more protein-rich baits after a long winter. Come April, they're often sick of maggots and search for something a little more appetising. Keep an eye on match reports and speak to locals because as soon as they switch onto meat, you'd be crazy not to follow.

Short is Best

Depending on the contours of the lake bed in front of me, my favourite

place to fish meat is on the short pole, usually at around four or five metres. On some venues I might choose to fish this line even closer, meaning yet again I'll be putting my plummet to good use.

I like to plumb up until I find where bottom becomes flat. At that point I'll come back on myself ever so slightly, looking to fish just up the slope on a hard bottom. Pushing out any further would mean fishing among the silt which tends to settle in the deepest water. Fishing on a silty bottom is best avoided if you can, typically leading to missed bites and foul hooked fish as they become preoccupied hunting through the silt.

On some venues at certain times, you can catch as short as a top kit in front. The positioning of your short line is yet again venue specific, so do some research and take your time while plumbing up.

Fishing meat on the short pole also allows me to throw bait accurately by hand, something that can be important when catching big weights of fish and looking to catch efficiently.

One thing which I love about meat is its slow sinking nature. It's this which makes meat so effective, leaving a trail of scent, fat, and flavour as it flutters through the water. With that in mind, fishing at close range also helps you keep the fish in your swim pinned to the bottom, where they're easy to catch.

Fishing with meat on the long pole in open water can be a deadly tactic when used 'up and down.' (I.e., with both shallow, deep shallow and deck rigs). However, this is the sort of method that you have to commit to, as you need to stay in touch with fish. The fish rarely settle at one depth all day, with the slow falling meat encouraging fish to feed at various levels in the water column.

So, for the sake of this chapter, we are going to concentrate on fishing meat on the short pole, which generally means fishing on the bottom. That said, on some venues which respond especially well to meat, you might have the opportunity to catch shallow even on your short line. Keep this in mind, particularly on heavily stocked lakes.

The Right Meat

A lot of anglers go to an awful lot of trouble when it comes to meat preparation. Some like to soak it overnight; others cover it in warm water. For me, the need for any such complication is avoided by simply buying the right brand of meat to begin with.

As I write, there are two kinds that I think are perfect. Plumrose, and Morrisons' own brand. What I am looking for is a meat that ▶

ABOVE:
Start feeding accurately via pole mounted pot. Once the fish start competing, you can start throwing some bait too.

BELOW RIGHT:
Diamond shaped floats have long been popular for meat fishing, especially in deeper water.

> ❝ *With water temperatures on the higher side, spring, summer, and autumn are often the best seasons to employ a meat approach.* ❞

ABOVE:
For some reason, meat has a habit of sorting out the bigger F1s and carp.

LEFT:
My preferred float pattern for shallow water - the RW Maggie. Note the visible, hollow bristle.

RIGHT:
A soft, hollow elastic like White Hydro or Preston 11 Hollo are perfect when mixed bags of carp and F1s are the target.

BELOW:
Throwing loose bait while playing a fish can be great way to make sure that there is one waiting next time you ship out.

is consistent in quality throughout the tin, firm so it will stay on the hook, and crucially, not too fatty - so it sinks when you throw it in water.

I use the MAP Meat Cutter, which has interchangeable blades, allowing me to use just one cutter for all my meat work. I cut my meat either the night before the session, storing it in polythene bags, or on the morning - putting some in bags, and some in a tub which I cover with a towel.

Immediately before use, I cover my meat in water, and remove any bits that float. I then drain the water off. This keeps the meat pink and fresh. I usually just fold a corner of the towel over the tub that I'm extracting bait from, ensuring the rest remains covered. If for any reason your meat has been left uncovered, don't be afraid of cutting up a fresh tin. Using dry, or crusty meat is a sure fire way of bringing fish off the bottom - causing a world of pain.

Diameter Decisions

When fishing meat short I tend to stick to three cube diameters and choose between them depending on the venue in question. On lakes dominated by F1s with an odd carp mixed in, 6mm meat must be my go-to. The perfect all-round size. Where more carp are expected to

get in on the action a 7mm cube would be my choice. On those venues where big carp into double figures are the target, I'll happily fish with 8mm cubes. A single millimetre either side might seem insignificant but trust me, it can make a dramatic difference.

I always cut the size that I think I need for feeding, and then do a few of the next size up for the hook, as sometimes a bigger piece on the hook can be a great way of bringing a faster bite or sorting out bigger fish.

Talking Terminal

My choice of terminal tackle largely depends on the venue in question. When F1s and small carp are the target, I'll opt for a relatively delicate approach. Starting at the elastic, I'll normally choose a medium hollow elastic, such as Preston Innovations'

> **" A bigger piece on the hook can be a great way of bringing a faster bite or sorting out bigger fish. "**

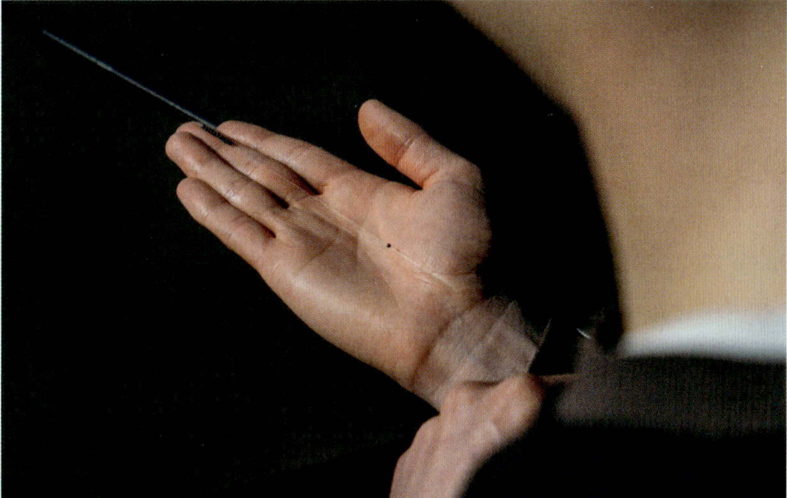

ABOVE:
Put your fish in the keepnet as quietly as possible when fishing at close quarters to avoid disturbing your swim.

RIGHT:
When the fishing is really good, a bulk and one dropper can be the best way to go, as it stops your bait being wafted around.

BELOW LEFT:
Hook your bait through one edge and out the other, leaving some point showing.

BELOW RIGHT:
Note the backshot just above the float. This helps keep the rig right where you want it.

11H or Daiwa's White Hydro in a long kit, either are perfect for landing fish of all sizes.

When choosing a float for fishing meat short, two patterns are universally popular. Some anglers, including some real greats like Steve Ringer, like a diamond shaped body, and visible bristle. Personally, I like a float with a slim body, carbon stem and a 1.7mm hollow bristle, offering a great compromise between buoyancy and sensitivity. With depth and the wind conditions in mind I'll choose between a 4x12, 4x14 or 4x16 RW Maggie 1.7mm float. A lighter float offers me a much slower fall of my hook bait, a real edge on certain days. On particularly windy days a 4x16 float would be my choice providing much greater stability. Line wise, like most of my other summer commercial rigs I'll opt for 0.17mm mainline followed by a 0.13mm or 0.15mm hooklength, again determined by exactly what I'm catching. If I'm bagging or catching a bigger average stamp of fish, I'll happily step it up to 0.15mm - but I'll never fish heavier than I need to.

In most situations, a six-inch hooklength will be my length of choice when fishing meat short, although if I'm faced with water shallower than 4ft I'll drop this down to a 4in. The Guru Kaizens are a popular hook for this style of fishing, as are the Guru SLWGs. A 14 would be my starting size but once again I'll adjust this to the fish I'm catching. ▶

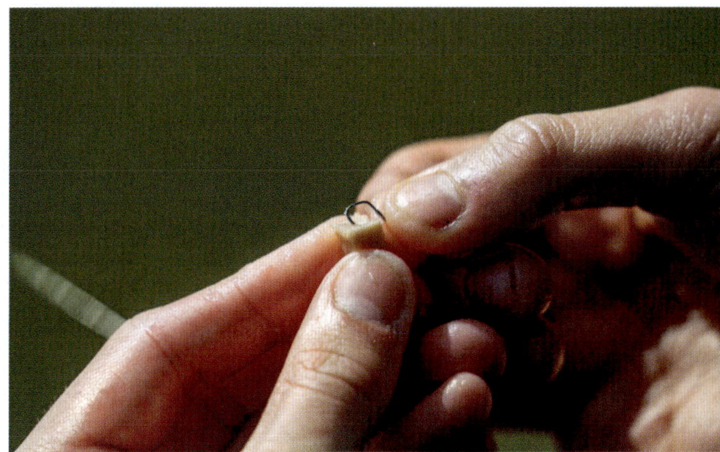

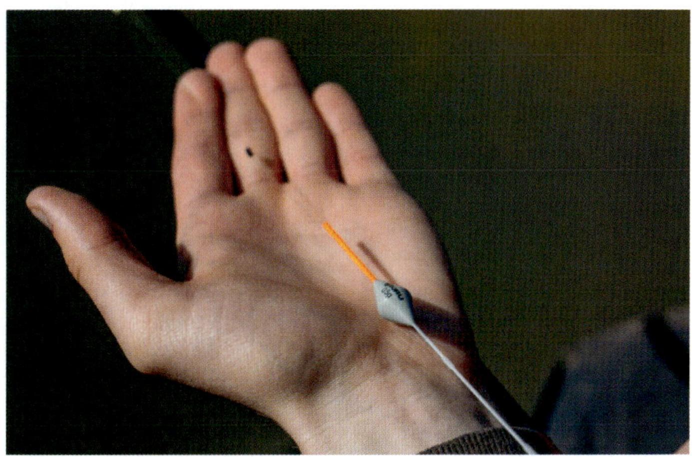

A bit of bristle showing is no bad thing when there are a lot of fish present, as it will help you decipher the bites from liners.

Finally, let's discuss shotting, the most important part of the rig in this instance. Since meat is such a slow falling bait, the shotting pattern reflects this. A simple bulk and two droppers are ideal to slow down the fall of the hook bait once near the bottom. I position my first No9 dropper shot at the top of my hooklength loop, followed by another six inches above that. You'll find my bulk of No8 shot a further seven inches above this to reduce tangles. This bulk is key to quickly getting the hook bait into the 'fishing zone' where most bites will come. The last two droppers then generate a slow fall of the meat in the final seconds before it settles on the lake bed. So many bites come right at this moment. The fish watch the meat as it flutters on by and drop in for a snack once it hits the deck.

When the fishing is really good, I will tighten this pattern up to a bulk and a single dropper. The advantage here is that it keeps your bait down, and stops it getting wafted around by moving fish, but still gives a bit of a fall into the killing zone.

Whether you're fishing for big bags of small carp and F1s or a few double figure carp, meat short can be a great tactic. For that reason, you must choose your terminal tackle carefully, scale my recommendations to suit the size of fish that you are targeting.

Nail Your Feeding

If you're to get the best from this line, it's vital that you get your feeding right. I almost always start my sessions feeding via a pole mounted pot. This ensures that my loose offerings land in super close proximity to my single hook bait. I find this particularly important when the fishing is slower at the beginning of a session, a point in the day when far fewer fish will be competing at any one time. Think of it as setting a trap, targeting one fish at a time. As the session progresses and fish begin to gather, I'll start to throw some loose cubes of meat around my float by hand. By creating a bigger spread of bait, it will in turn be easier to

> 66 *By creating a bigger spread of bait, it will in turn be easier to hold more fish in my swim at any one time.* 99

ABOVE:
Cover your meat in water, then drain and store in a covered tub to keep it in optimum condition.

BELOW LEFT:
The Guru Kaizen hooks are a great shape for meat fishing.

BELOW RIGHT:
The bigger paste pots can be better than standard size pole mounted pots for getting a quantity of bait where you want it.

hold more fish in my swim at any one time. The noise which this bait generates when landing will also pull more fish into the area.

When throwing bait like this you must be vigilant. It will often draw fish up off the bottom, causing line bites and foul hooked fish. If this happens, I'll alter my feeding pattern to suit. I might for example only feed by hand when my rig is not in the water, mostly when shipping back to land a hooked fish. This will prevent me striking at any false indications as fish intercept falling bait. By the time my rig is back in the water, most of the meat will be settled on the bottom. It's important to note that there aren't any hard and fast rules, the above is simply a guide - just be mindful of what you are trying to achieve.

How much I choose to feed at the start of a match is dependent on temperature and my knowledge and experience on that specific venue. For example, if temperatures were still cold overnight during spring, I'd begin cautiously, perhaps feeding four or five cubes of meat every drop in. As the fishing improves, I'll up my feeding to match. In general, my advice is to start off negatively and see how the fish respond as the session progresses.

in shallower water to use as your session progresses.

As mentioned, meat can be a devastating bait at times, and hopefully the tactics and concepts outlined in this feature will help you get the best from it. Always remember though, like worms, pellets, paste, and maggots, it's just another bait. When the fish are on it, it's amazing, but when they are not, being quick to change will keep your nose in front of the opposition. ■

LEFT:
Hold your rig out of the water and allow it to straighten over your feed before lowering.

Instant Bites

As I mentioned earlier, the slow fall of meat is a big part of its attraction so the way in which I introduce my rig reflects this. I'll first ship out to my desired position, pot, or throw my bait in and flick my rig slightly past. This is important considering I'm fishing on a slope. Without flicking the rig past, you run the risk of putting too much line on the bottom and missing bites as a result. I'll then hold my float

> **66 Once the line under my float is straight, I'll slowly lower my float down into position. An instant bite is highly likely so stay alert. 99**

around a foot out the water and once the line under my float is straight, I'll slowly lower my float down into position. An instant bite is highly likely so stay alert.

The Bagging Line

on certain days, when fishing particularly prolific lakes, meat short can work in really close proximity - i.e., on a top kit or shorter. As mentioned, it is one of those baits that the fish can go for crazy for, so when bigger bags of fish are on the cards, you might want to find shallow water and keep the fish pinned down to the bottom. Don't be afraid of starting your session at four or 5m and feeding a secondary line

LEFT:
Nailed right where you want him! Square in the top lip is a good sign your presentation is perfect.

BELOW:
Taking your time to be super accurate will bring quicker bites early on in the session.

THE BOMB
ATTACK!

The bomb is one of the simplest commercial methods out there - and with the right feeding approach it can also be the most deadly.

ABOVE: The bomb is a simple method, but the key to getting the most from it is mastering the feeding.

Like so much in fishing, straight lead or 'bomb' fishing is beautifully simple in concept. A lead, a bait, and the fish hook themselves against the weight of the bomb. A cynic might say even a complete novice could make the bomb work - and they can. But the truth is, it's the nuances of presentation and the feeding that can be the difference between catching a huge weight on the bomb and catching nothing.

Let's look at the advantage of fishing a bomb over other methods.

RIGHT:
The 'Paul Holland' rig, named after the man who showed it me. Note how the swivel will catch on the knot of the loop, causing some resistance.

> **❝ Many modern bombs are designed to enter the water with a plop which is not dissimilar to an 8mm pellet. ❞**

Firstly, its range. You can present a bait anywhere within casting range on a bomb - but realistically in the warmer months I only really want to fish it where I am able to loosefeed effectively, this means 30 metres

or less most of the time, which is considerably further than pole range.

Secondly there is noise - and I think this is often quite overlooked. Many modern bombs are designed to enter the water with a plop which is not dissimilar to an 8mm pellet. Plus, the way we feed on this tactic often sees an aggressive silo of big pellets raining down, which pulls feeding fish into the area.

Lastly, there is bite detection. Fished properly, there are only two types of bite on the bomb The fish is either 'on' (the tip pulls round and keeps on going) or it's not - you get liners, but no positive bites develop. This is a massive advantage over float fishing at times, as it stops missed bites and foul hooked fish.

Weston Lessons

Before I go into detail about how I fish the bomb, I want to talk about something I learned about this tactic during a visit to Weston Pools near Oswestry. I mention Weston specifically, as to look at it, you wouldn't think it was a bomb venue at all. Fairly small lakes, where most areas are easily accessible ▶

A standard 'free running' rig is used where venues insist on nothing above the bomb/ feeder.

with poles. But a few years ago, Giles Cochrane rocked up there, and began absolutely dominating the matches, simply fishing the bomb with 8mm pellets. He would often double pole anglers near him by simply casting his bait in, and feeding a pile of 8mm pellets tightly around it - then waiting.

Why? Because he was achieving perfect presentation, and all he had to do was wait patiently until a fish of the right stamp picked up his bait. Meanwhile, the anglers around him were suffering liners, foul hookers, and often catching smaller fish, too.

My point is, many anglers view the bomb only as a means of presenting a bait in parts of the lake that you can't reach with the pole, or in conditions when pole fishing is tricky – strong or gusting wind for instance. What Weston proved to me was that

> **66** *The bomb can actually give distinct advantages over the pole, even when you can fish it on an equivalent line.* **99**

the bomb can actually give distinct advantages over the pole, even when you can fish it on an equivalent line.

Tackle

There are lots of little edges to touch on here. Firstly, rod and reel choice. I like a soft, short rod where possible. I use my 10ft Daiwa Tournaments for most of this sort of work, matched with a 1oz tip. A

ABOVE LEFT:
Fat fingers? A pellet bander is a vital tool for fast and efficient banding.

ABOVE RIGHT:
Guru QM1s are my go to hook when big carp on big baits are the quarry.

RIGHT:
Hard pellets form the staple feed and hookbait - but other hook baits can give a dead edge too.

RIGHT:
Using a nice, short rod means that hooked fish pop up close to you, within comfortable netting range.

short rod gives lots of advantages in terms of accurate casting at close range, and also means that hooked fish will pop up closer to you, and you can often net them super quickly.

Reel wise, I'm happy to go for a 3000 or a 4000 size (the rod and reel are sitting in the rest most of the time), but a good drag system is vital. I will always set this fairly lightly to avoid being broken on the bite.

Line wise, I favour 8lb Daiwa Tournament or Guru Dragline. Something nice and robust, that can stand up to the pressure of playing fish positively.

The Rig

I'm going to touch on two here, my preferred option where allowed, is the 'Paul Holland' rig. This is a snap link swivel attached to the bomb and running on the mainline, down to a loop, with a link clip in it. The beauty of this is that, although it's free running, if you pull the loop through the eye of the swivel then there is a degree of resistance on the knot, so when a fish picks up your bait, it hits the knot and hooks itself easily.

Some venues are really strict however and insist that there is nothing at all on the line above the bomb – even the small knot. Here, I simply have the bomb running down to a leger stop above a loop, to which I attach my hooklength.

Hooks and hooklengths are among the most important

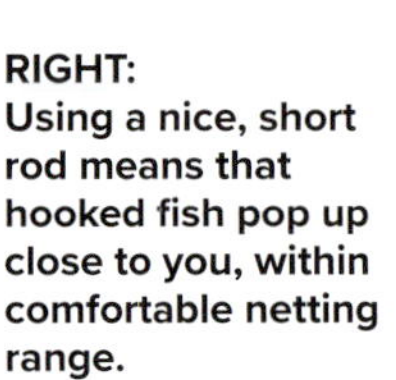

Wrapping hard pellets in bright Fjuka has brought some brilliant results in recent months.

ABOVE:
I often incorporate a small piece of silicone on the shank of my hook, so the pellet sits perfectly on the bend.

considerations when it comes to bomb fishing. I'm a big fan of the Guru QM1 hooks for a lot of big bait situations. When they go in, these simply don't seem to come out. They are supremely strong, and great for bagging. On tougher days, I do prefer a slightly smaller hook though. This is where the Preston KKMs come into play. These are lovely in both a size 16 and a size 14 for baits like 6mm pellet and a single grain of corn.

In terms of hooklength length, I go short in the majority of situations - eight inches or 12in. This gives the fish less chance to eject the bait than they have when fishing with longer (12in plus) hooklengths.

A final consideration is the bombs themselves. I carry a range of 15g, 20g and 30g bombs to suit the various situations that I find myself in. You always need to be able to tighten your tip so you know your rig is working properly, but my general rule is to fish as small a bomb as I can. The main reason for this is that little bombs make a lovely 'plop' as they hit the water, which imitates the sound of a pellet. With bigger bombs, it's a more distinct 'splash' which causes more disruption than attraction.

Feeding

Usually, a bomb approach is twinned with other methods, and where the wind allows, I will always fish a waggler over the same line as my bomb, to allow me to intercept any fish sat higher up in the water. In a match situation, there will often be a pole involved too, to fish the short pole or margins.

This is important, as having somewhere else to go and catch a few at various points in the match allows you to build your bomb line and optimise the amount that you catch.

While in the winter I might favour a corn approach, the summer sees two real feed baits come to the fore for me - 6mm pellets and 8mm pellets. Where allowed, I will have a tub of each on the side tray.

A good catapult is a must I like the big Preston or Guru models with the plastic pouches for getting the distance, but they don't half hurt your knuckles if you fire them wrong - so it's worth taking time to perfect your technique.

The 6mm pellets are great for laying down a bed of attractants and getting the fish grubbing around. But it's the 8mm pellets that I really want to work, as when you get the fish competing for these, you will find that bites come really quickly. ▶

LEFT:
Get your feeding right, and the fish will intercept tour hookbait with confidence.

LEFT:
A powerful catapult with a hard pouch will help you group baits at range... just watch those knuckles!

around the pellet, you suddenly create a bright, stand out 'conker' which can sometimes bring a really fast bite where other things fail.

Another useful tactic to nick a bite when you need one is switching to a really soft bait, like a double expander or big piece of

> 66 *Hooks and hooklengths are among the most important considerations when it comes to bomb fishing. I'm a big fan of the Guru QM1 hooks for a lot of big bait situations.* 99

punched meat. I imagine that the fish can suck these lighter baits in more easily, which is why they work so well on their day.

On some days it can be about constantly changing hook baits to get a reaction. On others you will simply sling out an 8mm pellet and catch on that all day.

Push them Down!

I mentioned briefly how I would start my peg off in terms of feeding, but I want to talk a bit more about how you can use the catapult to winkle out extra bites.

All you are ever trying to do when bomb fishing is drive fish

When good sized carp and F1s are the target, I will generally start by feeding 8mm pellets, and see what the response is. With any luck, you will find that the fish home in on them, and you can catch feeding these all day. However, if this doesn't happen, pouching in the 6mms can bring fresh fish into your peg, and get them feeding.

Hookbait

There are lots of little tricks that you can do with your hook baits to bring extra bites when bomb fishing, many of which I will touch on later, but my default position is always to try and 'match the hatch', so if I'm feeding 8mm pellets, I will fish an 8mm pellet on my band to start with.

When the fish are on it, it might not get any more complicated than this, but there are plenty of days when experimenting with, or varying your hookbait will bring better results than this one dimensional approach.

I have been using Fjuka baits effectively in these trickier situations. By moulding some Neeonz or 2in1

ABOVE:
Often feeding, then casting directly over your bait will bring a fast bite.

LEFT:
Robust mainline is necessary, as it will come under a lot of pressure on a good bomb session.

BELOW:
Although there not everyone's cup of tea, you can see why circle hooks (the QM1s) get such a firm hold.

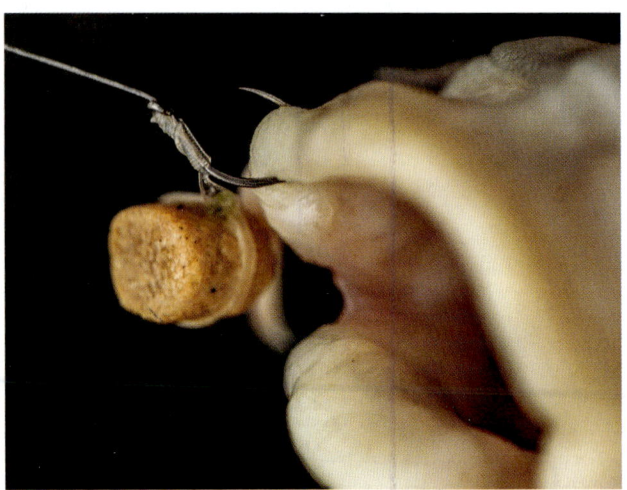

A lovely, bomb caught carp.

ABOVE:
The fruits of a busy few hours on the bomb.

down to the bottom, where they will intercept your bait.

Often on the good days its best to prepare your rod for the cast, then feed a pouch of bait, before casting your bait over the top of the area where your pellets have landed. If you do this promptly, you will get your hookbait landing on the bottom at a similar time to your loosefeed - and bites can often be savage.

> **I imagine that the fish can suck these lighter baits in more easily, which is why they work so well on their day.**

On some days, feeding just very lightly when you fish like this is the future, but on others, it's best to really fill the pouch with pellets. It's as if sometimes you have to feed a quantity of bait to make the fish feel like it's worth following your bait down to the bottom.

Rain It In!

Another deadly trick that works well at venues that specialist carp anglers visit regularly is to feed several pouches of bait (six to ten) in quick succession, then cast over the top and wait. I think this mimics the way carp anglers feed when baiting up, or pre-baiting. At times this can be a deadly way of fooling the bigger fish, possibly because there's no regular disturbance to the peg.

Finally, a couple of tips when it comes to bite detection. Firstly, either supreme patience, a butt rest or both are needed when it comes to bomb fishing. It's vital that you sit on your hands and wait until a fish

is unmistakably on before picking the rod up. I like to fish with only the slightest amount of tension in the tip, so I can read what is happening but there is less danger of any fish feeling a tight line and being spooked.

Watching when and how your liners occur in relation to when and how you feed can tell you a lot. For example, if your liners come straight after you feed, you know the fish are responding to it, and moving about to intercept it. On a deep venue, if you get big liners, it means the fish are closer to you, hitting the line higher in the water column, but little liners mean they are grubbing about on the bottom around your bomb.

It really is about using your quivertip as your indicator to fish activity as well as bites proper, and letting it influence your next move to generate a bite. As I said at the start, there is nothing complicated about bomb fishing - but hopefully these few pointers will give you some insight in to how to get the best from this deadly method. ∎

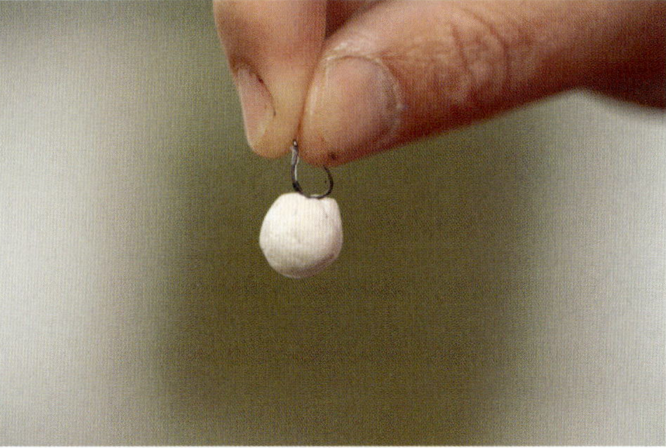

ABOVE:
A standout, white hook bit can be deadly on its day.

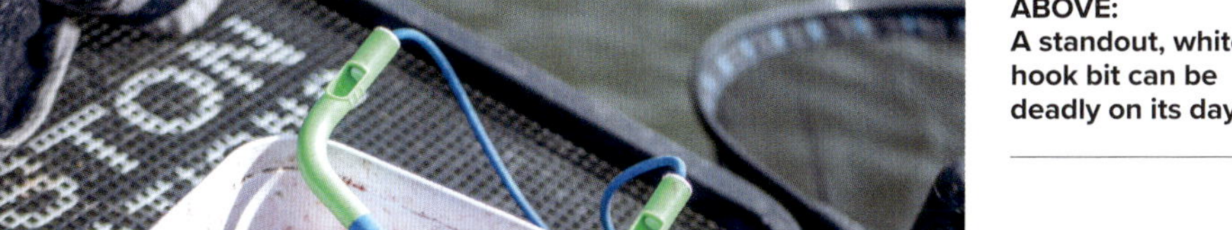

LEFT:
It's amazing how many pellets you can get through when attacking a bomb line. Eight to ten pints in a day is not unheard of then the fish are having it.

GET ON THE
WAGGLER

On its day, the waggler offers unrivalled presentation and fast fishing, leading to some massive hauls of carp.

With this being a publication about winning match fishing techniques, I haven't used the word 'fun' much. However, if there is one method covered here which is 'fun' it's the waggler. When conditions favour, and your setup is right, you won't find a more satisfying or enjoyable way of catching fish than this.

It's taken a lot of tinkering, playing with various products, as well as picking the brains of some of the best in the business to get me to a competent level here, as this is probably the most technically difficult technique covered in these pages. However, as with most running line fishing, practice definitely makes perfect - so if you've never done it before, I would definitely recommend a pleasure session or two to get your eye in.

I have also deliberately steered clear of the term 'pellet waggler', as although we may well use pellets as a bait (and this is covered in detail) it is sometimes unhelpful to think of the method in this way. As with any technique, there are days when pellets will work brilliantly, but there are also days when waggler and meat, or waggler and maggots will outscore little brown barrels.

Tackle

Rods first. There are countless rods labelled 'carp waggler' or 'pellet waggler', and sadly not all are fit for purpose. The biggest problem with many of them is the action, they are simply too stiff, or pokey. They feel great in the tackle shop - fast, responsive, and lightly balanced. But the truth is, choose a rod that's too 'tippy' and you'll be making life difficult for yourself.

While power is important, I like this as part of a progressive action, and although we don't need a ▶

> **" Choose a rod that's too 'tippy' and you'll be making life difficult for yourself. "**

A simple waggler set up, shown by **Preston Innovations** consultant, **Andy May.**

ABOVE:
Angry little commons like this give a great account of themselves on light waggler gear.

RIGHT;
Feed little and often to get the carp competing for your bait.

BELOW:
Note how the line is loaded right to the edge of the spool - this makes casting far easier.

rod for targeting carp and F1s to be super soft on the strike, I do like something that is forgiving in the tip, to avoid bumped fish.

Lengthwise, it's about matching the rod to the distance you are fishing. I use 11ft or 12ft rods for much of my pellet waggler work, but I will happily use a 13 footer if fishing at range. You are basically trading two sets of qualities off against each other when you make this choice; a short rod will land fish more quickly, and afford more accurate casting at short distances. A long rod gives more line control and will allow you to cast further.

I have a few rods in the armoury, but my favourite by some margin are the Guru Aventus waggler rods. I own these in 11ft, but also have 12ft and 13ft models in the armoury if I need them.

Reels next, and line. Firstly, I like a small, 3000 size reel for this busy style of fishing, as you are holding the rod a lot and casting in and out regularly. I use the Guru Aventus reels. These have an excellent drag system which comes in handy with the lightning fast bites that you sometimes get on this method.

Mainline Diameter

Reel line next, and this is again a real trade-off between two qualities, castability and durability. It's all about deciding which of these two is the most important for the type of water you are fishing, and then matching the reel line accordingly.

For most general work, I like 5lb b.s. Daiwa Tournament. This gives me the durability I am after, and I will happily use it for multiple sessions without changing. It means I can play fish with confidence - you would have to foul hook *Free Willy* in the tail to break this. However, the downside to this is that it doesn't cast as far, as accurately or perform as well in the wind as a thinner line would.

> **66** *As you might expect with a pre stretched line of such low diameter, it isn't as durable as its thicker cousins.* **99**

If the wind is behind me, or there is no wind at all, or if fishing at close range, I'm happy with this thicker line. However, if casting further or if fishing in wind, I am quick to scale down this mainline diameter. I really like the 3lb b.s. in the DH Angling Pro Match range as a next step down. This is still super strong, but casts beautifully. For ultimate presentation, for example if fishing for a handful of bites in winter on a breezy day, I will step down to Preston Reflo Power in 0.13mm. This is so good to fish with, and will land big fish easily, but as you might expect with a pre stretched line of such low diameter, it isn't as durable as its thicker cousins.

Float Choice

I'm going to talk about two diverse types of float here. For ease of reference, I'm going to call them 'muggers' and 'splashers.' The 'muggers' are all about stealth,

sneaking a bait in as naturally as possible, so it lands gently on the water causing no disturbance.

A 'splasher' is more of a traditional balsa pellet waggler; these go in a bit harder, and on the right day, the noise of them doing so will pull fish into the area. You need both in your armoury - but I find myself using 'muggers' far more than 'splashers' these days.

The 'muggers' are generally Styrofoam. The ones I use are handmade by Tez Naulls, who you can find on Facebook should you fancy ordering a few. The beauty of Styrofoam as a float material is that it doesn't dive deep if cast and set up correctly. I will come on to how to do this next.

> ## 66 The beauty of Styrofoam as a float material is that it doesn't dive deep if cast and set up correctly. 99

These cover 90% of my commercial waggler work. In winter, or if I'm fishing with natural baits like maggots, I might favour a standard crystal waggler occasionally, but the principles covered elsewhere still very much apply.

The Set-up

There are two ways I set up a waggler. The first applies to the splashers, and standard crystals. These are mostly pre-loaded, so

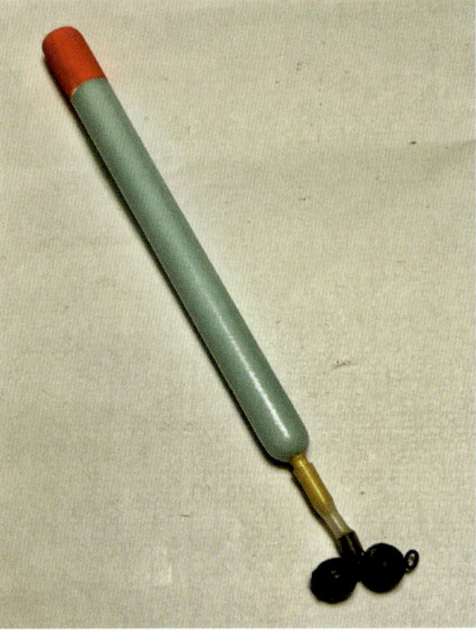

LEFT:
If you struggle to rebait with your fingers, a pellet bander will make life a whole lot easier.

LEFT:
One of my Styrofoam 'Tez Naulls'. wagglers. Note the adapter at the bottom, these are specific to each float.

no weight is needed on the line. I simply have two of the Guru super tight line stops above a Guru waggler adapter (to attach my waggler), and one below it. Set up like this, I simply move the stops up and down the line to adjust depth. Recently I have been experimenting with butting the bottom line stop up against the knot of the loop, which I use to attach my hooklength. This stops any sort of sliding of the waggler on the line and means that if I want to alter my depth, I simply shorten or lengthen the hooklength.

For the 'muggers' or Styrofoam wagglers, you have to sort out the shotting yourself. Two ways of doing this, the old fashioned way is simply to nip shot on the line around the waggler. If you do this, a good tip is to put more shot above the float than below it to cushion the fall. The second way of doing it is to make your own adapters. I do this by tying a 5mm rig ring on to the end of some power gum. I then thread the appropriate size Cralusso 'Globular' drilled bullets on to the power gum,

to make up the weights to shot the float, with the waggler in a float adapter located centrally on the line. Lastly, I melt a blob on the end of the power gum with a lighter, so it cannot pull back through. Again, this then attaches to a Guru waggler adapter, sandwiched between two line stops.

When it comes to hooks and hooklengths, three patterns tend to dominate. First up, the Guru QM1s, in my opinion, these are the ultimate carp bagging hook. I use these in a size 10 or 12, when there are a lot of big fish present. Next down is the Preston KKM. These are a smaller, finer pattern but still super strong. Use these in a size 14, 16, or 18 when mixed carp and F1s are the target. Lastly the old faithful Guru SLWG. These are used when direct hooking baits like maggots or Fjuka.

Hooklengths are tied to 0.17mm or 0.19mm Reflo Power, in lengths of two feet and three feet. ▶

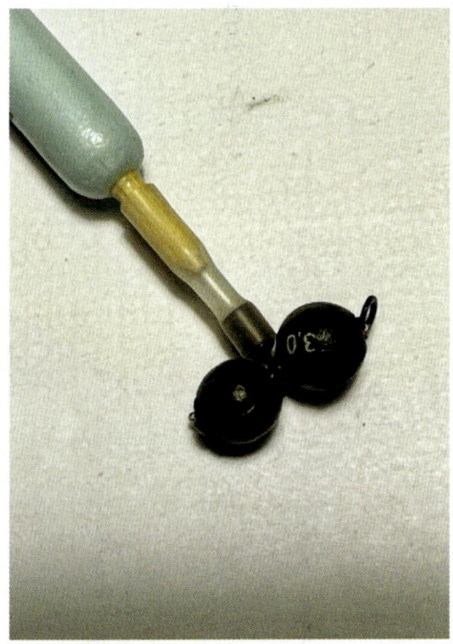

RIGHT:
Close up of the adapter.

BELOW:
5lb b.s. Daiwa Tournament is a real workhorse of a mainline, and perfect when bagging at close range.

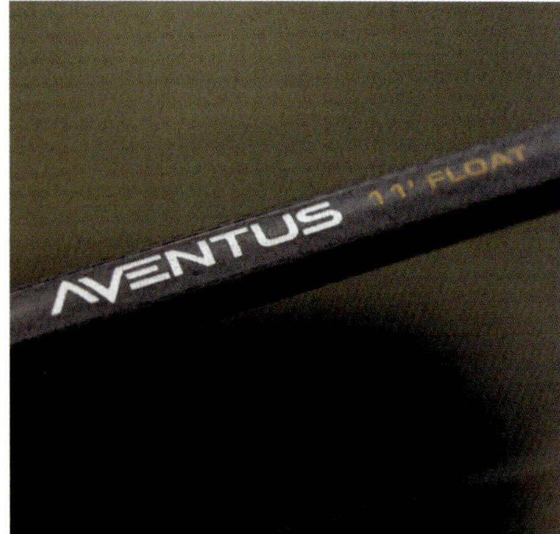

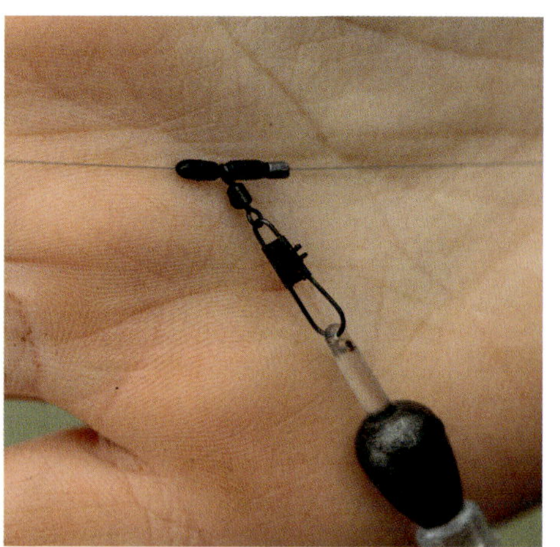

A Guru QM1 has been the downfall of many a waggler carp.

ABOVE LEFT: There are lots of great waggler rods out there, but the Guru Aventus are among the best.

ABOVE MIDDLE: I like some float showing, but not too much.

ABOVE RIGHT: If you are fishing in depths greater than three feet, or longer than your hooklengths, put a Stot under your bottom float stop to keep it in place.

got some power in reserve should the wind get up.

As with most kinds of fishing, the key to a great day on the waggler is getting the fish competing for food. This means regular loose feeding, little and often to get the fish looking up, and searching for their next offering. I will normally look to feed a swim for at least an hour before having a cast on it, just to make sure there are a few fish present and feeding.

> 66 *Some days, I will set a waggler rod up purely for 'mugging' or casting at fish which are showing.* 99

Mugging vs Feeding

Some days, I will set a waggler rod up purely for 'mugging' or casting at fish which are showing. Generally, though, it might be a combination of mugging fish, and catching fish in or around an area of feed. The bomb, or Method feeder is always also assembled when I'm doing this, as I like to have the option to present a static bait on the bottom, too.

Feed wise, its generally 8mm pellets when looking to build a swim in waggler range. A good catapult is needed, I like the big Drennan Waggler Range catapult, or the Guru Incredible Pult. As mentioned previously though, both can be knuckle bruisers if you don't get your technique right! I always like to fire pellets at a comfortable range in good conditions, so I know that I've

Regular feeding is crucial when building a waggler line.

When you do choose to go on the waggler, make sure you are ready for an instant bite. One mistake I used to make was to cast, then straight away attempt to feed. You miss lots of bites by doing this, often you will just have picked your catapult up and your float will be under. For this reason, keep your hand on your rod for at least the first ten seconds after casting, as this is when most bites will come. A great trick can be to feed, then cast straight into it, so

ABOVE:
Balsa wagglers definitely seem more stable in breezy conditions. Just make sure you can loosefeed accurately where you choose to cast.

ABOVE RIGHT:
It doesn't take many of them to build a winning weight!

INFLUENCER

There is only one angler to mention here, and he has not only improved my fishing with his knowledge of this area, but he has lifted the profile of commercial waggler fishing massively, too. That man is Andy Power. His attention to detail, rigs and technique have proved a real inspiration.

I mentioned fishing light in the feature, and this is one area that Andy has made his own. Very light mainlines, as fine as 0.13mm and tiny little Styrofoam wagglers allow him to tickle the surface of the water, tempting big, illusive carp into snatching at the bait.

'Mugging' on the waggler (casting at cruising fish) is also a speciality of his, Costa polarising sunglasses imported from America (also available at many UK fly fishing retailers) mean he can see fish others can't. He will often stand up for much of a session, just to allow him to spot more fish. A true waggler legend!

your hookbait is falling through your loosefeed.

Plop (Don't Splash)

Perhaps the most important skill to master when it comes to waggler fishing is the cast. You need to make your bait and float plop into the water. This is pure technique, but I can give a simple guide as to how I do it which should set you on the right path. Keep a couple of feet of line between the end of your rod and the waggler before you attempt the cast. Next, bring the waggler back behind your head and punch the float out. The natural tendency (and I know I used to be guilty of this) is to 'lob' the float, but you need

> ## 66 *Keep your hand on your rod for at least the first ten seconds after casting, as this is when most bites will come.* 99

to work to avoid this. The cast needs to be as direct as it can be towards the target, so there is no loop of line, as there can be when you 'lob' a cast. Just before the float hits the water, you need to feather the line on the spool with your finger - so the float enters the water with only the slightest amount of forward momentum, and the pellet lands on a tight line in front of it. Done correctly, everything from the rod tip to the bait should be tight on impact

with the water. Bites can often come super quick - so have your drag set loose.

Get the Rise

A great little trick to master is the twitch, or flick to make your hookbait rise then fall in the water. This can also prove a subtle way of straightening your line, if it has started to drift or bow after the cast. Keep your rod low and pointed at your float, and reel in three or four times, so that everything straightens.

To make this even more effective, combine it with a feed, so you are again pulling your hookbait back into the loose offerings. This gives you two bites of the cherry, in terms of presenting a falling bait among your feed every time you cast out.

So, a typical cast sequence might see you feed, cast into it, wait 20 seconds, feed, twitch the bait back into the feed, wait another 20 seconds and reel a carp in (or recast.)

Keep Busy

As you can see from that cast sequence, this is not a lazy method, you must constantly be casting, feeding, or playing fish to get the best from the waggler. Whether you are mugging or fishing in your feed, you need to keep one question in mind. Once your bait has been suspended at a depth for ten seconds, are you sure it's still working for you? If not, it's time for a twitch, or a recast. It might be you cast 200 plus times in a match to catch ten fish - but the beauty of the waggler is it can often sort out the big boys - and that might just be enough to win. ■

MASTERING
THE MARGINS

ABOVE: Deciding where in the margins to fish is often the million dollar question. Spare pegs often plumb up perfectly, giving a rock hard, flat bottom with the cover of the vacant pallet to mask your pole.

The first thing to say about margin fishing is that it has evolved quite a lot over the last few years. You will notice that we have split it across two chapters in this publication. The first - which I am covering here, relates to targeting big carp. The other, which is more specific to F1 type venues, deals with some tricks of the trade for catching big weights of F1s at close quarters.

I have structured the two chapters in this way quite deliberately, as the two approaches are often confused. I have had many a conversation with anglers about edge fishing who have been unable to get their head around the way in which the guy next to them has emptied it feeding only a palmful of bait, while they have blown their peg. It all comes down to the fish you are trying to target, and how you expect them to feed. On prolific F1 lakes, you might catch by feeding just a kinder pot of bait in the margins at the start of the session and repeating all day. But this chapter deals with older commercial fisheries, where you are often fishing for big, wily carp, and a more considered, but positive approach is needed.

This style of 'big carp' edge fishing probably plays a part in more commercial match wins every year than any other method. It also accounts for the most 'zero to hero' performances, as anglers can come back super strong with this tactic, amassing a big weight in super quick time.

Learned Behaviour

It's worth keeping in mind just why the margins work so well. It is learned behaviour for fish to move into this area of the lake at a certain time of day. When they come in here, they have one thing on their mind - and that is feeding. However, at most match venues

> **❝** *I have had many a conversation with anglers about edge fishing who have been unable to get their head around the way in which the guy next to them has emptied it feeding only a palmful of bait, while they have blown their peg.* **❞**

Catching big carp in the edge is one of the essential methods to master if you want to win on modern commercial fisheries. This is our guide.

they don't move in until late in the day - which is why the famous 'last hour' is so prolific.

The above dynamic is affected by two other factors, how many fish are present (competition) and how much they want to feed. This is why on, for example, a really good end peg, or on those few days every year when the fish go madly on the feed, you might actually catch down the edge for most of the day.

On most days, the edge is best only for the last couple of hours at  the most - and sometimes it might only be good for the last 15 minutes. Only experience at a certain venue will teach you this, and one key lesson I have learned the hard way over the years is that patience is key. If you aren't getting quick, regular bites on your edge line, it is probably best left alone and nurtured for later on in the session. I'm going to talk more about different feeding techniques later, but the real key with all edge fishing is building confidence, and getting the fish competing. It normally pays to put the work in nurturing the swim, so you can get the maximum return when you go on it.

TOP:
Take your time when landing big margin fish, once they are on the hook you need to make them count.

LEFT:
A good sized landing net is essential - double figure fish and bigger are common down the edge.

Depth Dilemma

Fishing in the right depth is absolutely crucial to getting the most from any edge swim. It can be the difference between the float flying under every time with a fish hooked in the mouth, and

Cover - or the lack of cover is another key consideration. If you are after two or three bites from big, wily 'crocodiles' then anything on the skyline, like a bush or platform is likely to be a big advantage in helping the fish move in with confidence. This is where 'gardening' (trimming the bankside foliage) can be a big help, as you can remove any obstructions that stop you getting where you need to be.

In the F1 margin chapter, I talk about how you can use yourself as a tool to keep the fish down near the bottom and catchable - and this same theory holds true here. If you are after a lot of carp, fishing up to clean, exposed banking - or coming

ABOVE:
Knowing where in the edge to fish is essential. Sometimes you might have to come a little way off the banking to find the correct bottom to present your bait on.

RIGHT:
Carrying a range of hooklengths is advisable. On tough days, scaling down will definitely get you more bites.

> 66 *In a nutshell, it's about thinking about what you want to achieve with your edge line, and locating it accordingly - while giving yourself options in terms of where to go.* 99

close to yourself can help keep the fish down where you want them, and stop your peg going too crazy.

So, in a nutshell, it's about thinking about what you want to achieve with your edge line, and locating it accordingly - while giving yourself options in terms of where to go - and not being afraid to change depths if the fish tell you to.

sitting there moving constantly with line bites, but never actually going under. I can't give a golden rule for this sadly as it varies massively depending on time of year - however I can give some particularly good rules of thumb which have served me over the years.

Firstly, when plumbing your peg look for a flat or slightly sloping bottom, ideally in close proximity to deeper water. The ideal scenario is that fish swim up from this deeper water into the shallows to feed. This kind of topography means that fish can feed with maximum confidence - as they have the sanctuary of deep water close by, but you also have the lovely slope, or flat dining area to present a bait well to them.

Time spent with a plummet exploring the margins is never wasted. If you are unsure what

depth the fish will be in, it can even be worth plumbing up a couple of likely looking areas in close proximity, so you can push up or down the shelf if you need to.

RIGHT:
A big splash may look dramatic and exciting, but I would far rather the fish swam out of the peg quietly, so it doesn't disturb other feeding fish.

Bait

A few years ago, there was something of a renaissance in margin fishing. Anglers started catching loads by 'big potting' groundbait down the edge. I had some great wins at White Acres doing this, as well as breaking my PB at the time with a 250lb net of carp from the Glebe. It was so beautifully simple. Mix groundbait on the damp side and top up with a full pot after every fish. For me, generally four or five dead red maggots were the hookbait of choice - and the carp LOVED it!

Fast forward two years and, well, they didn't love it quite so much anymore. The fish had wised up to the method, and though you could (and can) still catch on it, it wasn't the force that it once was. As the carp in our commercial waters evolve, they seem wiser than

ever- and finding the right bait to fish - that the fish want to feed on - is more important.

There are three main contenders for me. The first is groundbait.

ABOVE:
A puller kit means you can use light elastic and lines, but still bring the fish under control at the netting stage.

LEFT:
It doesn't take many of these to build a match winning weight!

BELOW:
It is better to nurture a margin swim until it comes to life than try and force it early. The fish will let you know fairly quickly if they are there and want to feed.

Although the days of really aggressive feeding as described above are gone, it is still a great attractor that I love to have in my armoury. It pulls fish in, and unlike particle baits which can be quickly hoovered up, there is always something left on the bottom to pull fresh fish into your peg when you feed some groundbait. Mix wise, I'm not too fussy as long as it has a good fishmeal and crushed pellet content. I always mix it on the damp side, so the particles sink and stay on the bottom, rather than running the risk of any popping up.

Next up is micro pellets. On venues where groundbait is banned, these take its place. They again provide that fine particle that you need to keep the fish grubbing about and in our peg.

> **"** *Sweetcorn is one of my favourite margin hook baits, and I always like to feed a fair bit too. When the fish are really ravenous, it can be that potting corn in keeps the fish down.* **"**

The third main feed that I have is actually the polar opposite of the first two - its big and heavy. Sweetcorn is one of my favourite margin hook baits, and I always like to feed a fair bit too. When the fish are really ravenous, it can be that ▶

LEFT:
Groundbait is my favourite margin attractor, laying down a super fine bed of particles.

RIGHT:
Preston 13 H is one of my favourite light margin elastics. Soft on the strike, but plenty of power in reserve to bring fish under control.

potting corn in keeps the fish down, and more easily catchable than the lighter particle baits. Indeed, a deadly tactic when it's like that can be to feed corn, and fish a light hookbait like a bunch of maggots on the hook. I always imagine the fish coming in and sucking, and your hookbait flying up and into their mouths before anything else.

In terms of hookbaits, again I have three favourites. The bunch of maggot I have already touched on, and single and double corn have been mentioned too. The third is a full dendrobaena worm or two, on some days fish will suck this in more readily than anything else.

Riot Gear?

There is nothing finer than those rare days when the fish almost give themselves up down the edge, and you can get away with the riot gear. Of course, strong lines, big hooks and heavy elastics mean you can land fish quickly and with confidence. I always set a top kit up to give me the option of doing this, too. My typical set up here might be 0.19mm Reflo Power to a 0.17mm hooklength. Float choice would be a

LEFT:
If a fish runs away from you, keeping your pole low, and at a slight angle is the best way to turn it, without risking a breakage.

BELOW LEFT:
The weight and brightness of corn make it one of my favourite margin hook baits. One piece is good, but sometimes, two is better.

BELOW RIGHT:
Guru Super LWG hooks in a size 14 are the go-to edge hunter.

> 66 *Elastic wise, for this kind of bagging I really do like to stop fish in their tracks - so a yellow Preston 17H or a red hydrolastic would be my choice.* 99

Mick Wilkinson Margin pattern, with a bulk at the top of the hooklength, and the hook would be a size 14 or 12 Guru Super LWG. Elastic wise, for this kind of bagging I really do like to stop fish in their tracks - so a yellow Preston 17H or a red hydrolastic would be my choice.

All the above said, we know that such halcyon day's edge fishing don't come along every time we go out. On tougher days, it might be more about nicking a handful of fish from the edge to get you over the line. So, I always like a lighter option set up too. We know how crafty the carp can be in our modern commercial waters, and I definitely think that fishing a little bit finer and a little bit lighter when it matters can render a big advantage. So I always have what I call a 'sensible' edge rig too. This will be more akin to what I might use for fishing long in open water, so typically 0.17mm mainline to 0.13mm hooklength, and a lighter, hollow elastic like a Preston 11h or 13h. Float choice is often lighter too, and on deeper swims, I'll use a more negative shotting pattern than the standard bulk. This little bit more finesse often means more bites, and fish in the net on tough days - and of course I have the riot gear set up and ready to go should I need it.

Keep Control

A final piece of advice. Because the margins sometimes take a little bit of time to get going, some anglers try and go into super high speed bagging mode as soon as they get a fish down the edge. As with all kinds of fishing, this rarely pays dividends. It's much better to be controlled, make sure you land what you hook with as little disturbance

ABOVE:
Frustratingly, margin fishing is definitely a tactic that is so much better when you are pleasure fishing and practicing than it is in a match - so don't get lulled into a false sense of confidence.

RIGHT:
Aggressive feeding with particle baits half an hour or more before you plan on going on your edge line should ensure that there is something there waiting for you.

RIGHT:
Marking inch long increments on your top kit can be invaluable in helping you gauge the depth quickly.

BELOW:
When the riot gear comes into play, you know a big weight is on the cards.

as possible, and most importantly of all, keep feeding. You will often find you need to reset the trap after every fish. Take your time and do this accurately. Then sit tight, until you get a positive bite, and make sure the fish is hooked in the mouth. More than ever these days, the finest of margins separate the winners from the also rans, and the fish that you hook down the edge are often the biggest of the day - so make them count. ■

F1 EDGES

If you're looking for success on well stocked, F1 dominated venues, you must be able to catch close.

ABOVE:
Ditch the big pots. Catching F1s at close quarters is all about bringing one fish in at a time.

With big carp edge fishing already covered in detail, this part of our handbook is set to focus on F1 edge fishing, covering all things close quarters.

If you're more familiar with the traditional, big-carp margin approach covered earlier, starting your match down the edge might sound alien, but trust me, when fishing venues which fit this approach, it can see an instant response.

It's important to remember that the fish in this type of densely stocked commercial fisheries are never far from the margins, often residing there all day long. Whether it's the start of a session, an hour into a match or with 30 minutes to go, on F1 dominated commercials the edges can be a fantastic place to target. If you can catch here, you can generally catch quickly, too - building a winning weight in no time.

RIGHT:
It takes perfect presentation to catch crafty F1s like this.

Where to Target

Knowing exactly where in the edge to target can be confusing and this varies hugely from venue to venue. With each season also requiring a slightly different approach, for the purpose of this chapter I'm going to focus on F1 edges during the summer months.

Depth wise, where available I like to start in around two feet of water down the edges, striking the perfect compromise. Not deep enough to be instantly inundated with liners and foul hookers but not shallow enough to deter any inquisitive fish from feeding. Remaining flexible with your depth is vital too, with the fish likely to behave differently as the day progresses.

As a rule, later in the session the fish will feed more confidently and in greater numbers ultimately requiring

> **Starting your match down the edge might sound alien, but trust me, when fishing venues which fit this approach, it can see an instant response.**

you to fish in shallower water to avoid foul hooking fish as they hunt for food. Keep your plummet within reach because I'd expect to use it multiple times throughout a match. On certain venues, you will have the luxury of a range of depths to choose from, allowing you to simply move up or down the sloping bottom accordingly. As I mentioned, two feet is a great starting depth and can be right for the entirety of your session. On other days, the fish will refuse to settle at one depth so changing to suit will be vital to success - and you have to let them tell you what to do.

Come Closer

If you aren't lucky enough to have drawn a peg with the luxury of depth variation, and you're in need of shallower water to help reduce line bites, this next tip is one you have to remember. By replumbing a new swim at closer range, you'll instantly reduce the number of fish coming into feed at any one time. Even in summer fish can be wary of anglers, so use this to your advantage.

F1 edge fishing requires efficiency, so the area of your swim you want to attract the fish to is something you must consider. Where possible, I like to fish within

five or six metres of my fishing station, enabling me to not only land fish quickly, but also ship back and forth efficiently when re-feeding. As I will cover later in this chapter, frequent feeding plays a big part in F1 edge fishing, so fishing at close range is important to make the process as smooth as possible.

When choosing exactly where to fish, there are a few things to look

ABOVE:
Get the fish going close, and a huge weight can be on the cards.

BELOW:
Catching close is a great way of ensuring that just the right quantity of fish come in at one time.

for. The first and most important is depth. For me this takes priority over every other consideration. The second thing I look for are features. If possible, I like to find my desired depth (usually 18in to two feet) tight against the bank or another feature like a pod of rushes. This helps to reduce line bites and foul hookers as any feeding fish will struggle to get behind my float and rig. ▶

Fishing against a feature also offers cover for the fish, something that can be particularly useful on hot bright days. Features also work as brilliant physical markers for your float, helping you easily maintain accuracy while fishing.

The Top Kit Line

A place which can often slide under the radar is the top kit line, one of my close quarter methods which is effective on venues up and down the country. F1s will happily come within touching distance during the summer months, particularly when tempted with a few loose offerings. I wouldn't expect to catch on this top kit line consistently, but it forms a brilliant resting line, allowing fish to build confidence on my other lines. Providing there's sufficient depth, usually around three to five feet, I'm more than happy to fish this line within a top kit's length of my platform, trickling bait there in preparation for a drop in at intervals throughout the day. You might only snare one or two fish when fishing this line, but I like to treat them as a bonus while resting other swims - and on other days it might throw up 30 fish!

Less is More

When it comes to F1 edge fishing, the volume of bait required to spark a response is minimal compared to big carp edge fishing, a little and often approach is far more effective.

At certain times through the day, I'll use my 100ml cupping kit pot to introduce a larger volume of bait, but for the most part my feed will be carried through small pole mounted pots. There really is no need to prime a swim when fishing down the edges for F1s, with the bulk of fish in very close proximity at all times. One small parcel of bait is often all that is needed to catch your first fish. I like to think of it as catching one fish at

> **On F1 dominated commercials the edges can be a fantastic place to target. If you can catch here, you can generally catch quickly.**

a time, looking to draw one fish into my peg, catch it and then reset my trap to hook another. Feeding an unnecessarily large volume of bait can cause chaos, drawing in too many fish at one time. A larger spread also makes it more difficult for a single fish to home in on your hook bait.

ABOVE:
Micro pellets are a deadly F1 attractor. I use these in deeper water, incorporating more groundbait if its shallower.

RIGHT:
If the going is tough, cutting your feed right back can lead to more bites down the edge.

BELOW LEFT: That lovely feeling when you sink the steel.

BELOW RIGHT: Take your time to plumb up as accurately as possible. Remember, F1s feed a lot more delicately than bigger carp - and you need to be able to see the bites.

As I have mentioned, pole pots are an absolute must for this approach, allowing easy control of feeding, while maintaining pinpoint accuracy. Like my summer mudline fishing, I have two main pole pots which form the basis of this approach. The first is a large Guru pole pot, a pot which I use when a greater volume of bait is required to draw a feeding fish onto my fishing position. If the fishing is very prolific this pot can be the best for the entirety of your session. However, on most occasions I'll need to bring the medium Guru pole pot into play, usually when I feel there is too much bait in the swim, resulting in feeding fish sitting in the peg while I'm playing and landing fish.

In an ideal world, I want to feed a small parcel of bait, draw a singular fish right under my pole tip, catch it and there to be no bait remaining exactly where I potted it. As a hooked fish kicks its tail, any remaining feed should be scattered, drifting down the slope forming a trail of attraction ready to guide the next fish into position. it's important to

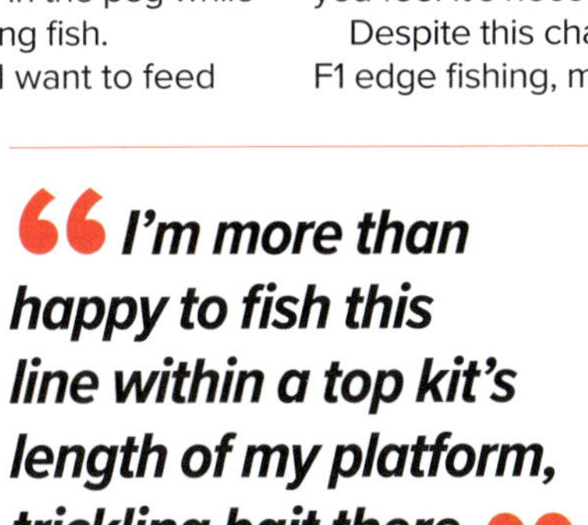

> **❝ I'm more than happy to fish this line within a top kit's length of my platform, trickling bait there. ❞**

be ready to change pole pots when you feel it's necessary.

Despite this chapter focusing on F1 edge fishing, most commercial fisheries which suit this approach will no doubt be home to many small to medium size carp too. For that reason, you must factor this into your approach, using the right pot for the feeding fish in your swim. With carp usually feeding more aggressively than F1s, the large Guru Kinder-sized pot is usually my choice when more carp are present. If I'm fishing for more F1s the medium pole pot is usually my go to once I have kickstarted my swim.

Generally, after a few feeds at the start of a session using my large 'Kinder-sized' pot, there will be enough scent and feed scattered in the area to hold fish as I swap down to the medium pot in the hope of managing the number of fish coming in to feed at any one time.

If action slows, a rest can sometimes be enough to reinvigorate your swim. At other times a rest combined with a larger volume of bait poured in can help attract some fish back to the area. I like to feed no more than 100ml of groundbait when resting a line ▶

in this way, a volume likely to be cleared quickly by fish as they start feeding. Once I drop back in with my pole rig, I'll start my process of trap setting once again.

Bait for a Weight

When fishing in shallow water down the edges, micro pellets and groundbait are the foundation of my approach, each offering different benefits which I can use to my advantage. Groundbait offers more attraction than micro pellets, but micros are a great holding bait and sink far more quickly than

> ❝ **The force created by a single swipe of its tail is enough to completely wipe out any remaining bait.** ❞

groundbait so are a must when fishing in slightly deeper water. A 50/50 mix of micros and groundbait offers me the best of both worlds, so is perfect when looking to start a session down the margins.

Whether you're feeding groundbait, micros or a mix of both, it's vital that you over wet your feed to ensure that it sinks quickly in one package to the bottom.

While predominantly feeding via a pole pot, a busy approach is crucial. You must remember that when a fish swims erratically through your feed area or spooks away from your pole tip, the force created by a single swipe of its tail is enough to completely wipe out any remaining bait. When this happens, it's vital that

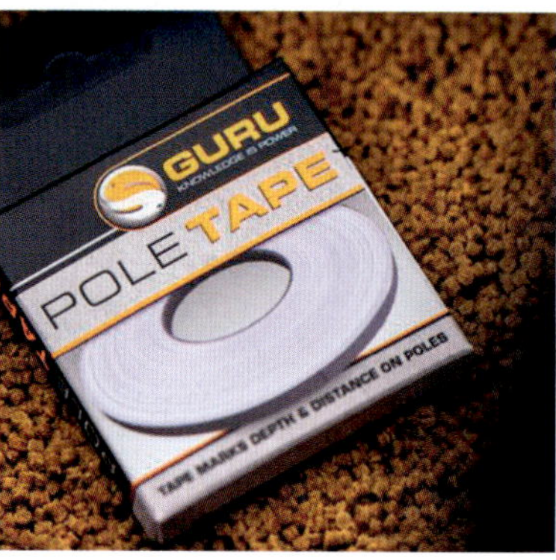

LEFT:
Accuracy is super important. Make sure you mark on your pole sections where you choose to fish.

LEFT:
Guru Pole Tape is perfect for marking depths on your pole sections, as you can peel it off straight after use.

you ship back, refill your pole pot, and reset the trap.

When fishing in deeper water down the edges or on the top kit line, a slightly different bait menu is necessary. Heavier particle baits are perfect here, sinking faster through the water column, helping keep fish on the bottom where they're far easier to catch. Baits like maggots, pellets and meat are always my go-to. Feeding little and often by hand while tending to different lines is the key here, giving you the opportunity to drop

BELOW:
If there are barbel in the lake that you are targeting, expect them to show up down deeper edges.

onto it when looking to rest other lines.

Let's talk hook baits. My number one when targeting the margins must be three live maggots. I don't find any need to kill maggots for the hook, although if your venue is especially populated by ravenous silver fish, I'd suggest that you take some dead maggots as a change bait. Corn, meat, and expander pellets can also be fantastic hook baits.

Scale Down for Success

A more refined approach is a must when targeting F1s at close quarters, there really is no place for heavy lines and big elastics, quite the opposite to my approach when targeting big carp down the margins.

Short top kits are one thing that I would never be without when F1 fishing. Not only do they help you land fish far more quickly, but they also stiffen up your pole considerably, important for hitting fast bites. Whether you're fishing for big carp or smaller F1s, using balanced tackle is a must! In most situations a white Hydro or equivalent is my go-to, offering enough stretch to allow fish to quietly glide out of the swim when hooked, while maintaining enough power in reserve to land fish quickly.

> ❝ **Short top kits are one thing that I would never be without when F1 fishing.** ❞

> ## *When fishing tight to a feature, hold your back shot right against it, pinning your float in position.*

I'll match this elastic with a durable 0.19mm mainline and an 0.13mm hooklength for finesse. As always, I like to keep a stronger range of hooklengths in reserve for use if some F1s and carp start to make an appearance. When fishing in less than two feet of water a bulk of shot right next to a short three or 4in hook length is perfect. In deeper water, a longer hooklength matched with a slightly strung-out shotting pattern (usually No9s) would be my preferred approach.

ABOVE:
The ideal scenario is that any carp or F1 swims out of the peg, washing away any other bait as it goes, so you never have a build top of bait.

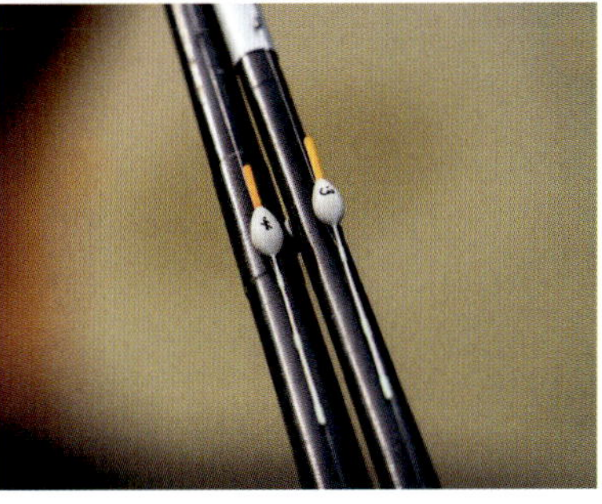

LEFT:
These RW Muddies are my choice for pinning a bait - though the Guru model in the other pictures is almost identical.

LEFT:
It's sometimes worth setting up different size rigs in the same edge, so you can vary presentation depending on how may fish are there.

'Muddie' style float is ideal, with a longer stemmed float better suited to deeper water. Hook choice is straight forward, and I reach for my ever-faithful size 16 SLWG from Guru, an incredibly sharp and strong hook that is yet to fail me.

An Unmissable Trick

Back shots are extremely important when fishing down the margins, helping you to maintain pinpoint accuracy. However, placement of these back shots above the float is crucial. I like to position two No8 shots two or three inches above my float, with the aim of preventing my float from drifting out of position. When fishing tight to a feature, hold your back shot right against it, pinning your float in position. You can't get any more accurate than that. ■

> ## *Stability is key when edge fishing, so a glass stemmed float is my favourite.*

Stability is key when edge fishing, so a glass stemmed float is my favourite. When fishing in water shallower than two feet, a stumpy'

INFLUENCER

Andy 'The Bagger' Bennett is a name synonymous with big weights of carp, F1s and silvers. The former FishOMania champion has really perfected this style of fishing and proved a real trendsetter. I have filmed him in matches many times, even when he hasn't looked to be catching, before proceeding to drop a big weight on the scales. An unbelievably smooth and efficient angler.

And it's this efficiency that is his biggest edge. Pinpoint accuracy when plumbing up to ensure he is always fishing on a nice flat bottom. Controlled feeding - so he brings the right number of fish into his peg at any one time, the patience of Job, so he doesn't strike until he knows a fish is on. And then smooth, calm playing of fish so almost every single one hooked ends up in the net. Get the little things right, and the big results take care of themselves.

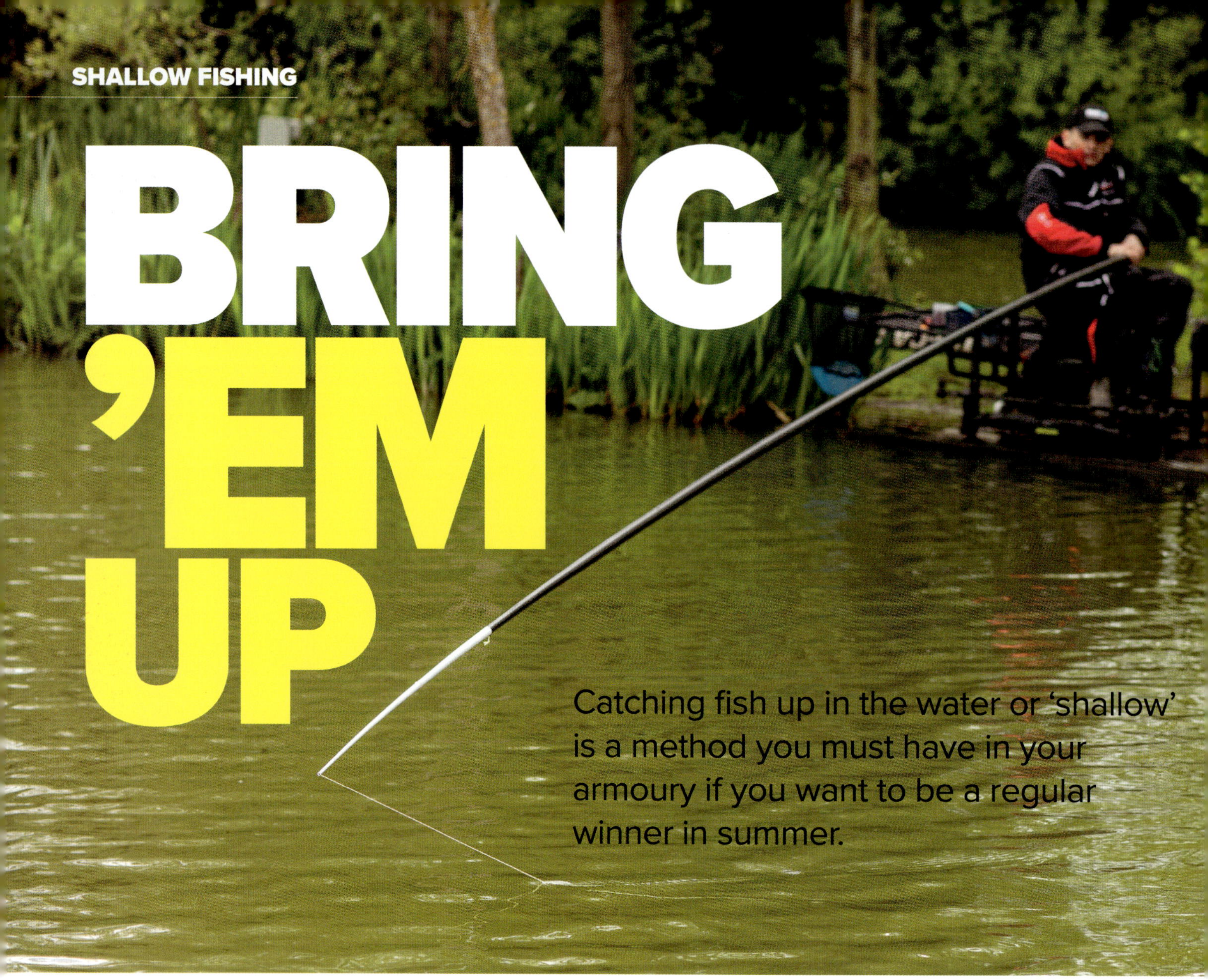

BRING 'EM UP

Catching fish up in the water or 'shallow' is a method you must have in your armoury if you want to be a regular winner in summer.

ABOVE: Shallow fishing is one of the deadliest summer methods, as it allows you to really get the fish competing for the bait.

Between the months of May and September, shallow fishing is responsible for countless match wins including many big money final qualifications. Why? Because it allows you to catch feeding fish quickly, and efficiently - get your set up right, and they will quite literally hang themselves on the end of your pole.

In a nutshell, shallow fishing involves regular loose feeding of maggots, casters, or pellets to create competition in your swim. This in turn will draw feeding fish to the upper layers where they can be caught quickly.

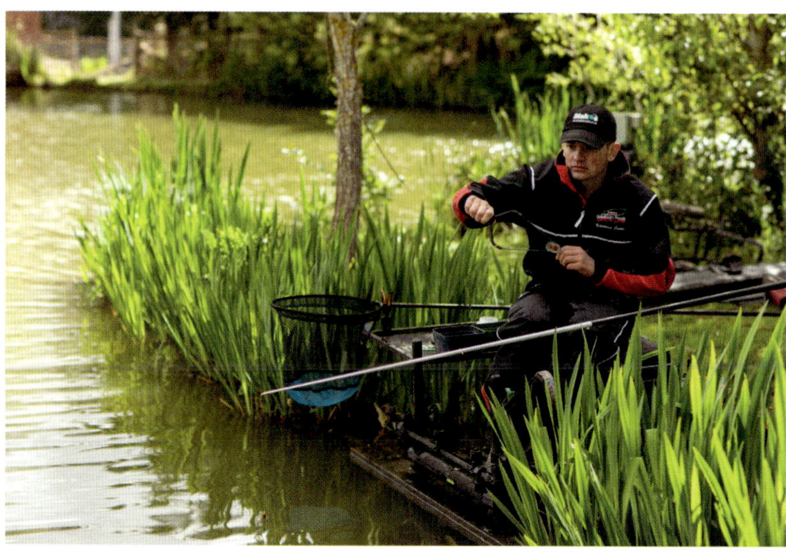

RIGHT: Effective shallow fishing is all about getting the fish competing and making your hookbait look natural among your feed.

Where?

Choosing the right venue and day to employ this method is crucial. In short, if the venue has a large head of fish, shallow fishing will probably be a match winner. If you're unsure of whether shallow fishing is the best way to approach a new venue, do some research before your visit. A quick look on Facebook or a call to the fishery is usually the best way to find out.

If you prefer a laid-back approach to your matches, this one isn't for you. Shallow fishing is quite possibly the most active of all the methods featured, with busier anglers always rising to the top - you should never be inactive if you are shallow fishing effectively.

The first part of any successful shallow fishing session is spent getting the fish competing. Granted, on certain red-letter days, the fish will be feeding like piranhas and minimal effort is required to get them feeding up in the water.

Accurate loose feeding is a must. The ideal formation is a tight area around, or slightly nearside of your float.

my falling bait in a much smaller area, I'll have more fish in one place, ultimately resulting in quicker bites as fish compete for bait.

Catapult choice is entirely personal. Find a couple which you like and learn how to use them effectively. Practice makes perfect. I like to have two in my arsenal for shallow fishing on the pole, one with a light elastic and one with a slightly thicker elastic for use if the wind gets up. The lighter of the two is always my go-to, enabling me to group my bait with minimum effort.

Bait for a Weight

The biggest misconception surrounding shallow fishing has to be the volume of bait required to win. Yes, certain venues can require large volumes of bait but on most occasions four or five pints will be more than enough. I would recommend four pints of bait as a minimum with a pint or two extra in reserve for those better sessions. On those more prolific days, you'll often feed less anyway, with more time spent playing and landing fish. The key thing is almost always ▶

> **Between the months of May and September, shallow fishing is responsible for countless match wins including many big money final qualifications.**

However, on many occasions it can take some time to build a swim full of feeding fish.

To do this, regular loosefeeding is a must. It might sound crazy, but feeding two or three times every minute is standard, creating a constant stream of bait falling through the water to bring the fish up.

I will rarely go straight on a shallow line; I'd much sooner spend some time building it up first and getting the fish feeding confidently.

Use a Catapult

Whether I'm fishing at five or 16 metres I always use a catapult when fishing shallow. The main reason for this is accuracy, with a catapult allowing me to group bait more easily around my pole tip. By concentrating

ABOVE:
When you are hooking fish in the top lip, you know your presentation is perfect.

RIGHT:
Puller kits are essential, as they let you fish soft elastics, but quickly bring fish under control at the netting stage.

BELOW:
Having the right length lash - or distance between your pole tip and float - will help you hit the greatest percentage of bites.

the regularity of feed rather than the quantity.

Three baits dominate when it comes to shallow fishing - maggots, casters, and pellets. Pellets are excellent when you're faced with a lake that's home to lots of newly stocked fish, which will have been reared on pellets since their early days in a hatchery. Pellets also sink far quicker than maggots and casters so are good on days when the fish are feeding so aggressively that they are intercepting bait an inch or two below the surface. The faster sinking pellets will help counter this by encouraging fish to feed further down where they're easier to catch. Pellets are brilliant on venues heavily stocked with small silvers too - when feeding natural baits might result in you catching the wrong species.

Maggots and casters both offer masses of attraction but choosing between the two can really make or break a session. In spring when shallow fishing is beginning to come to the fore, I'll always choose maggots. They also tend to be my choice on days when I expect the sport to be a little tougher. Colour wise, it is usually white maggots with an odd red mixed in as a change hook bait.

In the height of summer, when a really positive approach is required,

casters are my go-to. Their shape and structure mean they create more splash as they land on the water. Also, on days where there's a strong wind on the water, casters allow me to be more accurate than maggots, flying faster and straighter. Accuracy is everything. By the same token, casters are usually my choice when fishing at longer range, enabling me to still group my bait at 14 and 16 metres in tough conditions. Maggots can be great up to around 13 metres, but any further and your accuracy goes out the window, especially when conditions are less than perfect.

Hookbait choice is straightforward - you fish what you feed, but there are a few little edges that make a massive difference

> **66 Shallow fishing is quite possibly the most active of all the methods featured, with busier anglers always rising to the top. 99**

when targeting F1s and carp. When using pellets, the obvious one is a 4mm pellet, matching exactly what I'm feeding. When confidence is high among feeding fish, this is usually my choice. My second hook bait choice will usually be a Robin Red carp pellet in either a 4mm or 6mm diameter. With a slower break down, these oily pellets last a little longer in the band giving me the opportunity to land multiple fish on one hookbait. Their darker colour also makes them stand out, encouraging fish to home in on my hookbait among the many free offerings.

If maggots are my choice of feed, double maggot hooked straight on a size 16 is my go-to. This standout hookbait — two grubs - allows

feeding fish to pick it out much quicker.

Although I do direct hook on really finicky days, generally when caster fishing I fish a banded caster. As the name suggests, when I'm feeding casters, I'll use a band to secure a single caster next to my hook. I like to pick a slightly darker caster, usually one which I've kept out of any water to darken up. It might sound impossible, but once you find the right band it's super easy to gently push a caster inside. The best I have found are the Drennan Mini Bands.

Best Areas

Watercraft plays a huge role in match fishing success, helping you to select the best approach on the day. Fish love a ripple and will feed far more confidently up in the water under it, so if I was faced with a slight warm wind, I'd be very happy. By contrast, if it was a chilly May morning, and the lake was like glass, I'd be thinking that shallow fishing might prove tricky. Experience tells me that in this context, if I was going to catch shallow, the swim would need some nurturing, and the fish would more than likely be 'deep shallow' rather than right in the upper layers.

Fluctuating conditions through a match can also play a huge part especially in spring and autumn when it can be cooler at the start and end of the day. At times like this, I tend to find the shallow fishing is best at midday. Keep this in mind when reading your session.

Be Prepared!

Once again, preparation is super important with shallow fishing. Of course, there are levels to it and some of the very best shallow fishing anglers in the country win match after match with just two or three rigs to choose from.

For me, having several rigs to choose from gives me confidence. When fishing shallow, the fish are constantly moving up and down in the water column. This variation can be a result of a range of factors. These include

> **66** *On days where there's a strong wind on the water, casters allow me to be more accurate than maggots, flying faster and straighter. Accuracy is everything.* **99**

frequency of feeding, temperature, brightness, and the number of fish active in your swim. For example, if a ripple suddenly starts to form over your swim, any fish present might rise in the layers thanks to this additional cover.

It's very unlikely that you'll catch at one depth all day so having a good selection of rigs to choose from is a must. Let's talk about five key rigs which I wouldn't be without.

So, you're probably thinking why not just set a couple of rigs up, and slide the float up and down as and when you need to? The simple answer is that the length of line between your pole tip and float couldn't be more important, helping you control your rig and hit bites effectively. On most of my rigs, I'll use a four to 6-inch lash. Not so short that I'm constantly moving my float, but not long enough to cause frequent missed bites. Bear in mind, some fishery rules set a minimum lash length so check this before setting your rigs. In the same way, it's important that your lash length isn't too short. A lash which is too short could lead to you frequently moving your float out of position once it's slapped onto the water. By setting up more top kits you can avoid moving your float out of position, maintaining the optimum length of line between pole tip and float. ▶

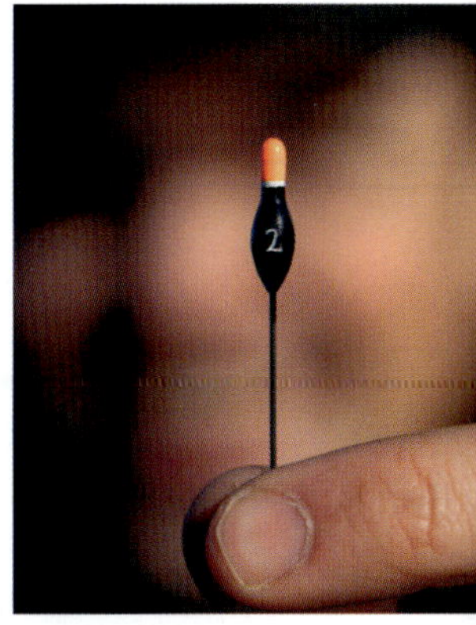

ABOVE:
These little RW dibbers are favourites in depths of a foot or less.

LEFT:
Carry two catapults - a softer one for most pole work, and something with a bit more 'grunt' in case the wind gets up.

LEFT:
If you have depth next to cover in the shape of a feature like a bridge stanchion then it can often make a great fish holding feature.

RIGHT:
When fishing pellets, I tend to stick to 4mm and 6mm hard pellets in the band - but an occasional change to an 8mm pellet can bring a bite from the blue. It makes a lovely plop as it hits the water!

LEFT:
As with most aggressive forms of fishing, it is the smoothest and most efficient anglers who normally come out on top.

BELOW:
I always tie my bands in a small loop, then whip down the shank so they lie next to the bend of the hook.

stringing out these shots is a subtle way to change your fortune. For most of my rigs, I'll use a three inch hook length but will opt for a two inch version when fishing less than 12in deep.

Since maggots and casters are lighter baits, they match up perfectly with more delicate floats. For fishing at 12in or less I'll employ a 0.1g dibber and for 12 to 14in, or when conditions are poor, I'll use a 0.2g dibber float. For rigs set above 15in I'll always use a bristled float. Something like the RW F1 Shalla or an AR float from Tackle Guru would be perfect. This enables me to read indications on my float and select a rig accordingly. False indications and missed bites are usually a sign that the fish are feeding shallower than the rig you're currently using.

It's also sensible to carry spares too, trashed rigs are a common hazard when shallow fishing. Being able to quickly replace one that's been tangled can save precious time.

The Rigs

Let's talk terminal tackle. The first four rigs measure from hook to float tip, each covering a selected depth. These include 12in, 18in, 24in and 30 inches. These six inch intervals allow me to swap between top kits and quickly chase the fish up and down the water column. In my opinion, the more top kits that you have at your disposal the better, enabling you to set up a greater range of depths at closer intervals. My eight ideal depths of choice would be 8in, 12in, 16in, 20in, 24in, 28in, 32in, and 36 inches. The closer my depth intervals, the more accurately I can locate the feeding fish, ultimately increasing my catch rate.

For all of these rigs my terminal tackle remains the same, with just a few tiny variations. Mainline is 0.17mm for durability, with 0.13mm and 0.15mm hooklengths at hand to choose between depending on the situation. The length of these hooklengths is something you simply can't overlook. F1s in particular are superbly crafty. They can easily suck in and spit out your hookbait without a bite even registering on the float. For that reason, using short hooklengths is key, allowing you to keep your final shot as close to your hook as possible. Shotting patterns for shallow fishing are dead simple. Most of the time I'll just use a bulk of number 10 shots right above my hooklength. This helps to magnify bites. If the fishing is a little tougher,

> **Having several rigs to choose from gives me confidence. When fishing shallow, the fish are constantly moving up and down in the water column.**

By the same token, a complete lack of indications is a sure sign that you're fishing too shallow. A swap to a deeper rig is usually all it takes to start catching again. When using pellets, it's important to slightly increase your float sizes, ensuring that they don't sink under the additional weight of the hookbait.

Where hooks are concerned there is only one size and pattern for me. The Guru 16 SLWG in a spade version for fishing with maggots and an eyed version for casters and pellets.

The 5th Rig (Bucking the Trend)

Prepare for some contradiction! Despite short lashes being vital in so many instances, I wouldn't be without my long line dibber rig. This rig is one which many people overlook. The rig features a 3ft lash above a 0.2g dibber float, allowing me to both flick it past my feed area and hold my pole high up off the water. It is fantastic in bright and hot conditions when there is minimal wind on the water. In these conditions fish can be particularly spooky. Bigger and wiser F1s will also sit at the back of your feeding area, making this rig perfect for picking them off throughout the day. Think of it as a way of nicking the odd big, wary fish throughout the session.

Making Noise

Making noise, often referred to as ringing the dinner gong, plays a huge part in catching big weights shallow on the pole. Feeding fish associate splashes with food entering the water, so using disturbance correctly can tip the odds massively in your favour. Slapping or turning your rig over is the most common way of making noise, creating the widely talked about 'double plop' of your float and hook bait. Tapping your pole tip on the water is another way of making noise and can be particularly deadly when there's a significant ripple covering your swim.

These tricks are a must for your armoury but be careful not to use them at the wrong times. Slapping the rig repeatedly or tapping the water on flat calm days could spook any feeding fish and be detrimental to your catch rate. On some days, a simple lift and drop of your rig is all that is required to induce a bite.

As with all styles of fishing, it's about working out what the fish want as you go, but hopefully the principles and tactics outlined above will give you a fighting chance of some red hot shallow action. ∎

ABOVE LEFT:
Banded casters prove more resilient than when they are simply direct hooked.

ABOVE RIGHT:
A rig with a longer lash can often fool bigger fish from the back of the feed area.

ABOVE:
When maggots are the bait of choice, two whites are a deadly option.

LEFT:
On tricky days, moving the bulk shot into a strung pattern can bring extra bites.

DECKING IT!

Long pole fishing on the bottom is one of the most common techniques that you see used in commercial matches. So how do you get an edge if everyone is doing it?

This technique has probably won me more commercial matches than any others that we have covered. It is also what I might term a 'bread and butter' method. It can be used alongside anything else covered here to winkle out a few fish when you need them, and as such confidence that you can 'catch long on the deck' is vital.

The most common difficulty encountered with this method - the 'stick in the mud' if you will excuse

the pun - is the makeup of the lake bottom. On most commercial venues, a build-up of fish excrement, leaf mould and leftover bait has led to a thick bed of silt. This means that presenting a bait on the bottom on the long pole can be troublesome, as the fish eventually bury into this soft bottom, leading to line bites and foul hooked fish. So a lot of what I talk about here is actually about managing this, and keeping fish coming when fishing on a soft bottom.

To start with though, I want to deal with the opposite scenario - the perfect, hard gravelly or sandy bottom! Some venues (often the ones that get flushed through by a natural watercourse) are like this, and when you land on one, and the fish are feeding well, they can be an absolute treat! They also, in my opinion give you a good understanding of how fish feed - which you can use to influence what you do elsewhere, perhaps where the bottom isn't so perfect.

So, the first, key piece of advice would be to take some time to try and find the hardest bottom that you can find in your swim. If the venue you are on has aerators, fishing towards them can be very good as they generally blow away any silt. Other lakes have shallower, raised or gravel bars. If you can find one, happy days! If you can't, hopefully my advice in the second half of the chapter will prove useful.

LEFT: The catapult is a deadly tool but use with care when fishing on the deck as you want to keep the fish down.

A Nice, Hard Bed

For the sake of simplicity, let's presume we are talking summer fishing, and have found a lovely hard lake bed to work with. The key objective is getting the fish where you want them and getting them competing for food. However, what you also need to be mindful of is getting too many fish in the ▶

BELOW; Fishing the long pole on the bottom is one of the most consistent year-round methods for keeping bites coming.

ABOVE: It's worth taking the time to make sure that your seatbox is set up properly, so your feet are flat on the footplate. You can soon hurt your back fishing long if your setup isn't correct.

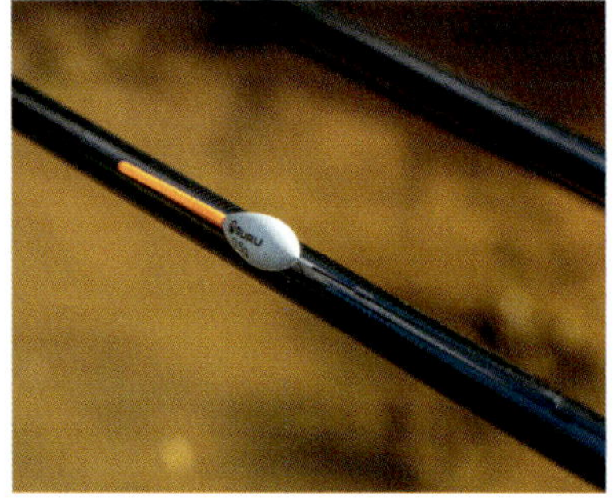

RIGHT: The MW Pinger is my choice when fishing for big fish on nice clean bottoms, when you can leave some bristle out.

feeding on a hard bottom here where the bait introduced will stay put, feed this amount on a soft lake bed, and it could be match over.

The beauty of feeding with a big pot like this as opposed to with a pole mounted or 'Kinder' pot, is that the bait has an amount of time to

> ## 66 If the venue you are on has aerators, fishing towards them can be very good as they generally blow away any silt. 99

peg, or bringing them up in the water, which makes them tricky to catch. The ideal scenario is that you keep a few fish pinned to the bottom, grubbing around looking for food, and maintain this level of competition through the match.

There are three ways of feeding - a big pot, a pole mounted pot, and a catapult - and all three will probably come into play at some point during an event.

Generally, though, I like to kick off with a small amount of bait fed via a big pot. I also like to feed a variety of different size particles - so if I'm fishing meat, it might be half a handful of hemp and half a handful of meat, or if its pellets it might be half a handful of 6mm pellets and half a handful of 8mm. It's important to stress again - I'm talking about

settle on the bottom while you ship back, take off your cupping kit, and ship back out with your top kit on. I always imagine fish rising up to intercept your bait, then following it down, and by the time you are back out there lowering your rig in, the fish are settled and feeding.

For fishing on this kind of nice, hard bottom I will use an MW Pinger float, with around half an inch of bristle showing, so I can read what is going on beneath the water's surface. Shotting will be a bulk and two droppers, and I will have an 8in hooklength with two or three inches of line on the bottom. Expect a few line bites when fishing for big fish

RIGHT: Big, open water venues often hold good heads of skimmers too, which are always welcome.

Fish balanced gear, and even big fish like this should come in with ease.

> **There are three ways of feeding - a big pot, a pole mounted pot, and a catapult - and all three will probably come into play at some point.**

in deep water, there are a lot of fins and tails wafting around, and the key is to wait for a fast, sharp bite.

Again, sticking to our ideal scenario, if bites come straight away, I'll fish the initial deposit of bait out, i.e., not feed again until I stop getting bites, then repeat the process with a similar amount of bait.

On days when it goes like this, the fishing is lovely, as by feeding just with the big pot you can keep control of your peg, and keep the fish where you want them.

As we know though, fishing rarely goes as we plan, and is more often about having to adapt to variable amounts of fish at different parts of

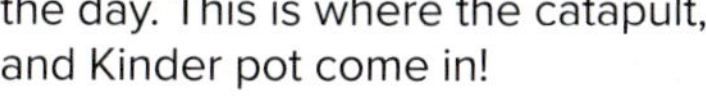

ABOVE LEFT: When a big fish is hooked it can pay to lift your pole and bring it up off the bottom when fishing over silt, this keeps disturbance of your swim to a minimum.

LEFT: Slimmer, more sensitive floats like this are generally my choice when fishing over silt.

LEFT: These medium Guru pots help me keep fish pinned to the bottom, by feeding a small volume of bait in a clump, that the fish can then follow down.

the day. This is where the catapult, and Kinder pot come in!

The Power of Noise

So, take the above as the ideal scenario, because we have kept the fish pinned to bottom. Picking up the catapult is a way of bringing fresh fish into the peg - but we have to be careful not to get giddy.

Noise, and bait falling through the water can literally turn a devoid swim into one with some promise. The key is to manage how you use the catapult, keeping that aim in mind - i.e.- we need to keep the fish down.

Going back to our above scenarios, say I waited ten minutes over that initial feed and never had a bite, I would then pick up the catapult and start trying to draw fish in. I would loosefeed two or three bits of bait every couple of minutes, until things started to happen.

Often, this works a treat - and as soon as you know the fish are responding to it you can progress your match. Unlike say, shallow fishing where you are trying to pull fish up and get them competing, think of the catapult in this context as a tool to attract fish into the area.

RIGHT: Sometimes, a big change-bait, like this Fjuka Fatboy can bring an instant response.

LEFT: A black marker pen is an invaluable tool to the long pole angler. Sometimes, when the light's bad and you're fishing in open water glare it holds the only chance you have of seeing your float.

Once they are there, it might be that we go back to big potting, or use the pole mounted pot to feed little bits of bait regularly, but without the noise factor.

On some days of course, the fish will want loosefeed, and it will be a case of feeding only by catapult, but trying to keep the fish pinned down. In this instance, I sometimes like to feed twice with a quantity of bait every couple of fish to force the fish down, rather than loose feeding little and often once the fish arrive.

The Kinder Pot

The pole mounted, or Kinder pot is a brilliant way to introduce small amounts of bait right around your float. As mentioned at the outset, the majority of venues that I visit suffer from a build-up of silt on the bottom - which means you have to tread very carefully when it comes to bait and feeding.

> ❝ **The Kinder pot often ends up being your best friend on a lot of silty venues when fishing long on the bottom.** ❞

For this reason, and the above perfect scenario aside, the Kinder pot often ends up being your best friend on a lot of silty venues when fishing long on the bottom.

Where silt is concerned, it's much better to feed a little bit of bait, then see how the swim responds to it. Literally two, or three pieces of bait is often all you need to instigate a response - and

it's much better to 'starve them on to the hook' in this scenario. Often, after catching a few fish over silt, you will find you have to move lines, and start again on a clean bottom.

> ❝ **Picking up the catapult is a way of bringing fresh fish into the peg - but we have to be careful not to get giddy.** ❞

LEFT: Carry a couple of different sized plummets, a big one is useful for finding silty areas, and a smaller one for fine tuning where you are actually going to fish.

BELOW: Guru SLWGs (spade) are the ideal hook for long pole fishing on the bottom. For hard pellets, I use the eyed version.

The beauty of the Kinder pot is that it allows you to be super accurate, while still being minimalist with the feed, and using a sprinkle lid, you can work and rotate several lines in the same depth without constantly shipping back to refeed.

Pinging

Another deadly tactic - which gives you the best of both worlds in terms of minimalist feeding and noise attraction is a tactic that we call 'pinging.' This involves pinging via catapult one or two pieces of bait at a time to instigate a response from passing fish.

The beauty of this is that is prevents the dreaded build-up of bait, which I mentioned earlier, while giving all the advantages of noise and bait falling through the water.

Best fished with big pellets or meat, this tactic used to be absolutely deadly at White Acres, and still scores well at a lot of venues to this day.

Tackle

Catching on the bottom over silt requires a different tackle approach to catching on a clean bottom - and sadly the positive ' bristle out' approach I described above doesn't always score so well. The truth is, when faced with silt it's not just us that don't like fishing on it, the fish don't particularly like feeding on it either.

The key to success is generating bites as your bait settles, so light floats, and shotting that encourages your bait to fall nicely through the water is the order of the day. Depending on the depth, I would go for a 4x10, 4x12 or 4x14 RW Maggie. Shotting wise, I would either use a strung bulk of No10 or No11 shot covering the last two feet, or a bulk and two droppers depending on how good the fishing was.

Because that fall through the water is so important, I would also be prepared to experiment with hooklength length. Sometimes, the

A final tip when it comes to catching on the deck, that was passed onto me a few years ago by Andy Geldart. Never be afraid to try a BIG change bait. Some years ago, this was a deadly edge at White Acres. Fishing 6mm pellets, it was regular bites from small F1s and skimmers, put an 8mm pellet on and all of a sudden you would be into a carp. It didn't work every time - but three or four fish nicked on this through the match often made a big difference come the weigh in. More recently, I've had success doing this same thing with Fjuka Fatboys. The fish just seem to home in on that big, soft bait. ■

free fall given by using an eight or 12in hooklength as opposed to a six inch one can prove a big advantage.

Look for Bubbles

Perhaps the only positive to fishing on silt, is that the fish do tend to betray their presence by fizzing. So you can often tell when fish are

> ❝ *Never be afraid to try a BIG change bait. Some years ago, this was a deadly edge at White Acres.* ❞

feeding on the bottom because there will be small bubbles rising to the surface, over the line. If you see them over one of your swims, drop in. If you don't get a bite, be careful not to become preoccupied though, as it can be very easy to be drawn into chasing shadows.

ABOVE: If the fish will only respond to loosefeed, sometimes 'double pouching' (feeding twice , then fishing it out) is a good way of keeping the fish down.

RIGHT: When fishing at long lengths, the stiffness and responsiveness of a more expensive pole really starts to become worth the extra investment.

BELOW: Leaving a bit of bristle showing will help you read bites when there are multiple big fish feeding over a volume of bait.

INFLUENCER

Andy Geldart helped me massively with this style of fishing as a younger angler. His knowledge and understanding of how commercial carp feed is among the best I have ever known, as his results at White Acres (and his FishOMania win) prove. In particular, the tips passed on here about a big change bait, and the use of long hooklengths has led to some great results for me.

HIT AND HAUL

ABOVE:
When the paste goes, it can be unbeatable.

Paste fishing is one of the oldest commercial fishery methods out there - but I can't help thinking it is turning into something of a forgotten art on many venues. The truth is, there are a lot of downsides to this method. It's risky - there are times when it simply doesn't work, pulling in the wrong fish and leaving you striking at thin air. It's also messy - a day on the paste can often see you walking off the bank looking like you have been rolling around in mushy peas. And it can be almost unrivalled in its ability to frustrate anglers, with foul hooked and lost fish galore if you don't get it quite right.

That said, it is also unrivalled in its ability to amass a huge weight really quickly. There are times when double figure fish will suck in a ball of paste, but not touch any smaller particle bait. And the best thing? You can get away with big lines, hooks, and elastics so you land the fish super quickly.

Perhaps the best example of this from recent years was down at White Acres. Four anglers in particular, Carl Williams, Tony Evans, Tom Edwards (pictured) and Kevin Wadge built up a deadly reputation for winning their sections (and often the lake) in the dying stages of the match with huge fish on paste. Kevin Wadge even won the

£25,000 Parkdean Masters final on the stuff - and I got a ringside seat being just a couple of pegs down from him. He landed some massive fish in super quick time, and frankly, made the anglers around him look a bit daft.

So, we have established that paste has almost unrivalled match winning potential on its day. It's also fair to say it can be a bit of a boom or bust method though. In fact, I would go as far as to say anglers who rely on paste exclusively will bomb out more often than they do well. The key is - as anglers like those mentioned above have proved - you have to build paste into a varied attack, and not

LEFT:
Green Swim Stim is a firm favourite of mine for paste - and also the go-to for many top anglers.

BELOW:
Plenty of bristle helps you read true bites from liners.

When it comes to amassing huge weights of big carp quickly, paste fishing is a deadly technique.

> **A day on the paste can often see you walking off the bank looking like you have been rolling around in mushy peas.**

become preoccupied with it. This way, you can harness its match winning potential, without risking the house on it working.

Tackle Up!

To be totally clear, this chapter is about targeting big weights of carp on paste. There are other adaptations to this method, like the so called 'pea paste' that some anglers use for F1s, but here we are talking about targeting carp.

There really is no need to fish fine when it comes to this sort of work. Big hooks, big lines and big elastics are the order of the day.

A strong, but relatively fine hook is best, as the efficacy of ▶

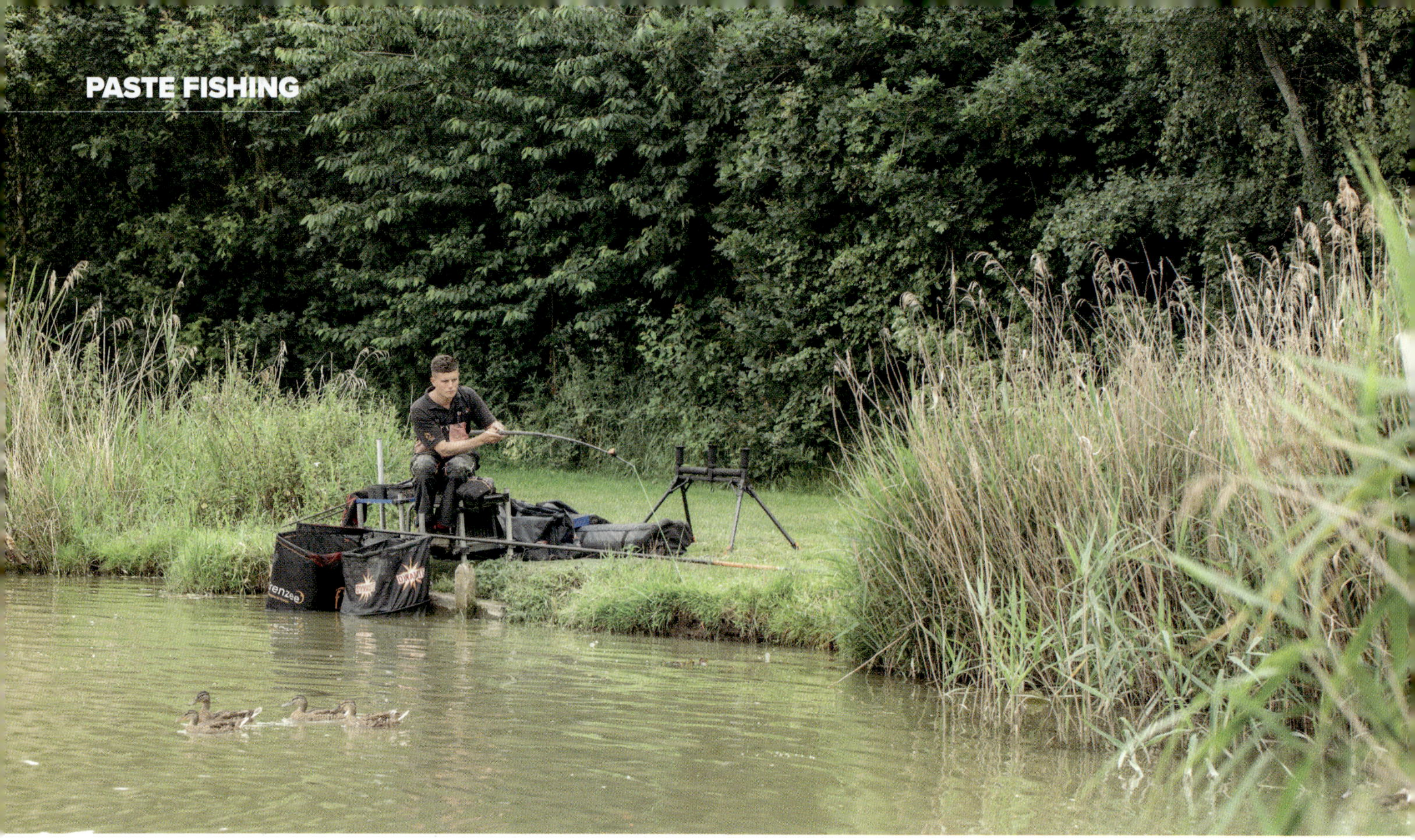

ABOVE:
Few methods sort out the bigger fish as well as paste.

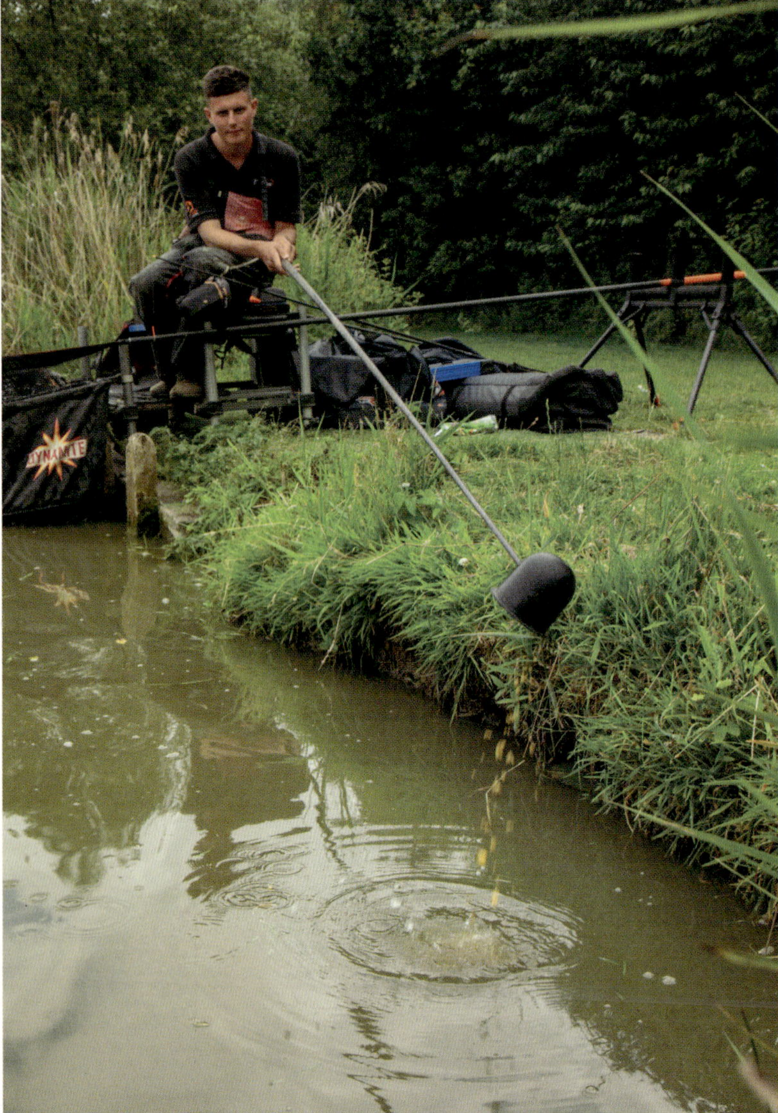

LEFT:
Regularly potting in particles helps to build the paste line before you go in on it.

BELOW:
Keep introducing a few particles each time you ship out to keep fish grazing.

the method hinges around the carp sucking in a pile of bait (with your hook in the middle of it.) The Guru Pellet Waggler pattern in a size ten or 12 is my go-to. I tend to match this to a 0.19mm hooklength, with a mainline of 0.21mm or higher. Strength is vital, but you also need the ability to change your hooks, as they sometimes do blunt when

> ***"I would go as far as to say anglers who rely on paste exclusively will bomb out more often than they do well."***

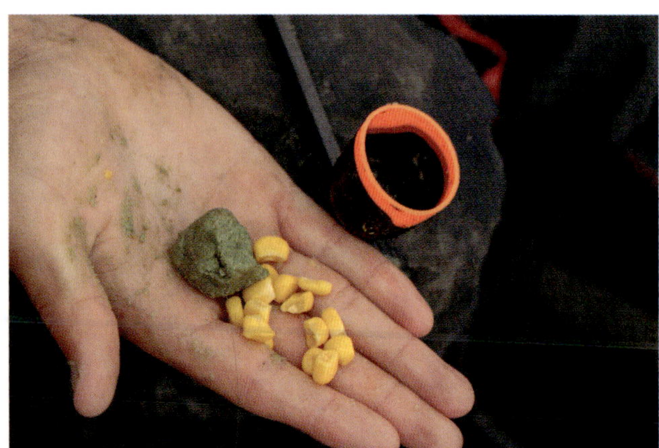

a very soft paste. It wants to be just firm enough to be mouldable around the hook - but certainly no firmer.

In terms of other baits, I always take 4mm pellets, corn and (if

> **When it comes to the float, strength is vital - as is a long, visible bristle. This will be the key when deciphering the proper bites from any liners or false indications.**

> **There really is no need to fish fine when it comes to this sort of work. Big hooks, big lines and big elastics are the order of the day.**

you're bagging - so I always like to incorporate a hooklength rather than fishing straight through. Elastic is red Hydro or similar, Preston's No17 Hollo is also a great choice. When it comes to the float, strength is vital - as is a long, visible bristle. This will be the key when deciphering the proper bites from any liners or false indications.

In depths under four feet, I like a 4x12 float with three No8 shots down the line, in a simple bulk 12in from the hook. And that's it! Simple, strong, and effective.

Where to Fish

If there is one thing to get right to when it comes to paste fishing it's where you choose to fish. Obviously, every peg and venue is different but there are a few guidelines I would always try and stick to. Firstly, you need a hard bottom. If fishing in the edge, this is rarely a problem, as it tends to be clay or gravel here.

When fishing further out in the lake, it's very important to take your time with the plummet - as the harder the bottom the easier the fish will be to catch. Often, a top kit or top four kit will be plenty close enough. The ideal in my opinion is a slight slope, so the fish move in from deeper water and suck in your bait from a nice, firm dinner plate. Ideally, I will also fish at an angle away from me, so fish can be hooked, then guided away from the area where I have hooked them and then netted.

Paste

Stories of secret pastes abound in the match fishing world, and of course certain flavours always work better at specific venues. For me, there are two key things that need to be right though -flavour and consistency. I personally use Dynamite Baits Green Swim Stim as the basis for my paste fishing. I mix it the night before the session, as I want the particles to have fully absorbed the water - otherwise, your paste will be drying out through the session. Consistency wise, I'm after

ABOVE:
The trap is set...

LEFT:
The Guru pellet waggler hooks are both fine and strong - so perfect for paste fishing.

allowed) hemp when I'm looking to fish paste. These are used to make some noise, and create a little carpet of particles around where you are fishing, then the paste is the focal bait that any carp that enters the area just has to suck in!

Timing

More than ever, our commercial fisheries seem to run like clockwork, with experience you can often ▶

RIGHT:
Robust hooklengths are a must.

BELOW:
A conker sized piece of paste generally proves about right.

ABOVE:
Simply push the hook into the paste, give a little twist, then squeeze.

LEFT:
A puller kit is vital - helping you bring big fish under control quickly before netting.

BELOW:
Don't spare the horses when it comes to the strike - you will have to rebait anyway.

you commit to striking you are going to have to come back and rebait anyway, so you can afford to let them have it!

Smooth and Low

A quick word on playing fish. The key to landing big fish quickly on heavy gear is all about making the fish come towards you, and then tricking them into the net. When the fish bolts away from you after you have hooked it, keep the pole low to the water, it won't be too long before your elastic tires the fish, and its head is turned back towards you. The key then is shipping back smoothly. No need to rush, just keep the fish coming in your direction. Once you're down to your top kit, I always like to get at least one good strip of elastic off the puller kit, I look at this as my

tell almost to the minute when the carp are going to move in and start to feed. For me, this is when I will go on a paste line. I want to know that the big fish are feeding.

I will have primed the area where I am wanting to fish paste with my loose particles for at least an hour before I go on it. In my head, this builds the peg, getting the fish used to feeding in the area that you are looking to target.

When I go on the line, I will have a large pole mounted pot to house my paste. I will then add about 50ml of particles, with my ball of paste on top - and feed the lot in one dump. A conker size piece of paste is generally about right for match sized carp, you want a good dollop with your hook in the middle of it.

> **66** *Crucially, I set my rig so the weight of the paste registers on the float. In other words - the rig is slightly under-shotted.* **99**

Crucially, I set my rig so the weight of the paste registers on the float. In other words - the rig is slightly under-shotted, so the paste pulls it down in the water. I like having a bit of bristle out the water, as this helps me read bites from liners, but it's very important you can read on your float whether your paste is on (i.e. the float sits slightly lower in the water) or off.

Once the trap is set, patience is the name of the game. Obviously experience is key here, but basically any fast, sharp pull under is a bite. Ignore any little dips, lifts or drags - these are line bites. You will soon come to realise that proper bites are pretty much unmistakable. I like a firm strike when paste fishing. After all, once safety margin, so if any fish bolts away from me I can release this and add sections. All being well though, I keep the top kit low, and bring it round to the side slowly, which makes the fish swim right in front of my keep net. I then quickly but smoothly, turn the top kit so its pulling the fish upwards, and often the head will pop up, and into the waiting net.

This of course is the perfect scenario, and it's not always this simple. But with practice, you can make this system work the majority of the time, and land big fish in super quick time.

In and Out

One key piece of advice with paste fishing is not to waste any time, I literally spend two to three minutes maximum in the water, before striking my paste off, coming in, and repeating the process. Some days, if bites are coming quickly, it's even less than that.

I look at this as a very aggressive method, so if I'm not getting regular bites, I will quickly be off it and doing something else.

If I suspect paste will work, I will keep building the swim though by potting in the particles-remember the positivity of this method means it doesn't take long to build a winning weight.

When the paste swim comes to life, you will find you are getting regular, clean bites, while constantly building your peg - and building a match winning weight in double quick time. ■

LEFT:
With the right playing technique you can bring big fish under control in no time.

BELOW LEFT:
A lovely paste caught carp

BELOW RIGHT:
Proof of the pudding - a big net of carp on the paste.

EFFICIENT
THINKING

Catching big weights of fish isn't all about speed. There are a few key things that can really help you keep your nose in front of the opposition.

Have a landing net set up that's big enough for anything you are likely to hook - but also one that makes unhooking the 'match sized' fish easy.

The standard of match fishing in the UK has never been higher. To keep your nose in front of the pack, it's important you fine tune your kit, so you are as efficient as possible on the bank.

The aim of this chapter is to bounce a lot of ideas around about tweaks to your setup that can really help your efficiency.

Let's start with the obvious one - your seatbox setup. It's so important to get this right, not just so you can land fish as efficiently as possible, but also for your comfort on the bank - and if pole fishing, to prevent you from injuring your back.

I like a level seat, with my knees at a right angle to my body. I use an Octbox D36 and concede it's a very expensive choice. However,

in its defence I spend more time sitting on it than I do on my sofa so from that perspective, it's a good buy! Crucially, my feet must be level on the footplate, so they can support the weight of my pole. In most situations I like two side trays - I have the Octbox big side tray to my left, and behind me I have a smaller tray. The one to my left is the one that I work with while sat on the box, and given the adjustable posts on the D36, I am able to set this to just the right height, so I can comfortably reach my bait while fishing. The tray behind me can be used to store extra hook boxes, my flask or anything else that I might need, but which doesn't need to be immediately to hand.

To my right is my pole sock if pole fishing, or butt rest if feeder fishing. For the pole, I love the Guru pole sock, as it features two pockets, and a handy tulip-like grip if you push the two pockets apart. This is essential for keeping everything where you want it, especially when it is windy.

Moving further back, there are my rollers. I LOVE the Matrix Flatbed rollers, especially when used in conjunction with the adjustable legs. These allow you to set the height to almost whatever you want, up to and including six feet tall if

you so desire. The option is brilliant when you have a drop or awkward bank behind you.

Importantly, I like to be able to ship back with the pole low, but never touching the water, and when I unship the top kit, know that I can whack the discarded sections in the pole sock without looking - so I can fully focus on what the fish is doing and make sure he ends up in the net.

Moving onto nets, one area that is often overlooked is landing net head size. There are two key thoughts here. I want to be able to land everything I might hook, so ▶

> ❝ *To keep your nose in front of the pack, it's important you fine tune your kit, so you are as efficient as possible on the bank.* ❞

ABOVE:
Your feet should be flat on your footplate so you can easily hold the pole while catapulting out bait.

LEFT:
Where multiple nets are required, the new short (2.5m) keep nets are perfect - and make sure you put them all in at the start.

I will always set one net up that is big enough to allow me to do this. However, if fishing for a number of fish, I also want a net head size that allows me to control the fish that I have hooked quickly. There is nothing worse than trying to lean to the bottom of a huge, deep net to retrieve a small fish. So, I will use a shallowish pan for match sized fish, that allows me to bring whatever I have caught in easily, and importantly, control it and unhook it quickly when it's in the pan before transfer to the keepnet.

A final point on landing nets - if you are fishing with a band, hair rig, or quick stop, always use a 'hair' net, too. The fine mesh of these prevents your hair falling between the gaps in the mesh and snapping off. They also prevent the front barb of a carp's dorsal fin snagging.

Keepnet Management

A few years ago, this wouldn't have been worth a mention, as at most venues it was just a case of whacking a couple of nets in and splitting your fish between them. Not any longer! On some matches these days, you need upwards of four nets, and if you get your net management wrong, at some venues you risk total disqualification from the match.

Touch wood (and I'm doing so as I type) this has never happened to me, but I take a very safe view. I always start the session by putting in the most nets that I think I will need. So it might be that 200lb has been winning matches at a set venue, with a 70lb net limit. I will put four nets in at the start and split my fish between them. This way, if I fill them all, I have comfortably caught enough to win. But the chances are, I am not going to come close to filling them - and even if I have 50lb in each one, I still might win.

> **I love the Matrix Flatbed rollers, especially when used in conjunction with the adjustable legs.**

There are also benefits to this approach in terms of the fishing, too. There is nothing that I hate more than putting an extra net in while I am catching, especially at close quarters, for example if I'm catching short or down the edge. This can really disturb the swim; I've had it kill lines completely in the past. So I'd far rather look a bit silly come the weigh in and have 20lb in each net, than risk

ABOVE:
The Matrix Flatbed Rollers have turned into one of my favourite items of tackle. They are shown here with two leg extensions.

BELOW:
FishOMania winner Kristian Jones and I use the same top kit configuration. The long kits are the same length as a Daiwa top two and the shorter kits are just under two metres long.

whole host of advantages when it comes to playing and landing fish quickly and efficiently. Firstly, because there is only a short length of elastic in them, there is no need for endless stripping of elastic at the netting stage - you can simply ship back, pull a couple of strips of elastic out and net the fish. This is also kinder on the elastic; you will find that you don't have to change it as often.

Secondly, because of their shorter length, the fish pop up closer to you when you lift at the netting stage, making netting easier.

And finally, you can store them with the rigs on, ready to go - brilliant when you need quite a few set up when it comes to shallow fishing.

All the above said, I do like some longer kits too. These standard length top kits are just under seven feet on my pole, and come into play when open water fishing for a mixture of carp and F1s. It's definitely possible to have too little in the tank in terms of stretch when it comes to short kits, so if it could be a 2lb F1 one minute but a 15lb carp the next, the longer kits are always my choice. ◾

ABOVE:
The Guru Reaper pole sock is a great tool - two socks either side and the gap in the middle acts as a tulip grip.

RIGHT:
If needed, I'll mount a pole or rod roast off the rear backside of my side tray.

FAR RIGHT: I have used the Octbox system for years now, and honestly believe its among the most stable and adaptable fishing stations out there.

RIGHT: I like a fine mesh landing net the fishing with bait bands, spikes, or hairs. This helps to prevent the hair rig snapping while fish are writhing in the net.

going over, or spooking feeding fish by slipping an extra net in mid-match.

In terms of how I fill them, to me the simplest and most logical way is to rotate around, so I start with my left hand net, and work round in sequence.

The Right Top Kits

A final point on efficiency relates to top kit length. I appreciate that not everyone can afford to have

multiple top kits for their pole, but if you can, I think it's worth a thought.

The short kits that are so popular these days are perfect for most applications when small carp and F1s are the target. They offer a

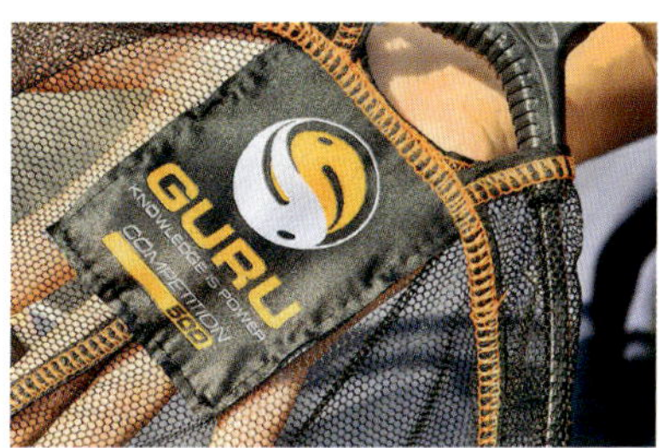

Britain at War is dedicated to exploring every aspect of Britain's involvement in conflicts from the turn of the 20th century through to the present day.

shop.keypublishing.com/bawsubs

Classic Land Rover is an exciting monthly magazine dedicated to Series and the classic Land Rovers.

classiclandrover.com

Airfix Model World magazine is your complete guide to the world of scale modelling. Catering for all manner of modellers, from the eager novice to the experienced master modeller.

keymodelworld.com/airfix-model-world

Hornby Magazine takes a unique approach to model railways with both the relatively inexperienced and the seasoned modeller in mind.

keymodelworld.com/hornby-magazine

Order direct or subscribe at:

shop.keypublishing.com

Or call **UK 01780 480404** Overseas **+44 1780 480404**

Lines open 9.00-5.30, Monday-Friday

253/23

WHEN IT PAYS TO DO NOTHING

Feeding no bait at all might sound negative, but 'dobbing' is a proven winter winner.

ABOVE:
Many people think dobbing is best done to cover, but in truth some of the best days can be had by targeting open water.

RIGHT:
The Guru bread board is a dobber's best friend. It keeps your bread fresh and stores your punches where they can't get lost.

f you're a tight Yorkshireman like me, this method will be right up your street. When dobbing during the winter months you don't need to feed a bean, a few hookbaits are all that is required for a potential red letter day. So, what exactly is dobbing? Dobbing

> " **Dobbing is a method of finding and catching fish using single hookbaits without feeding any loose offerings for attraction.** "

is a method of finding and catching fish using single hookbaits without feeding any loose offerings for attraction.

With dobbing, It's down to you to find the fish, as opposed to when you feed bait and they come

to you - in theory, anyway. This method certainly isn't something I would employ all year round but it shares some qualities with mugging carp during the summer months – casting to (or laying your bait in front of) a visible cruising fish.

Why Does It Work?

With water temperatures so low during winter, fish are far less interested in feeding than they are in the warmer months, often only tucking into an odd morsel during the closing stages of a session. They also often shoal tightly. Dobbing enables you to catch the fish that are sat in front of you, but not necessarily feeding, without running the risk of pushing them out of reach, a problem often encountered by match and pleasure anglers during the winter.

ABOVE:
Place the bulk of shot under the float for stability, with just a couple down the line to give a slow fall of the bait.

LEFT:
A soft, hollow elastic means fish will swim out of your peg without causing undue disturbance - which means the rest of the shoal will stay in your swim for longer.

BELOW:
Aerators can be a good place to start your search when it comes to fish location.

Coupled with cooling water comes the problem of water clarity. Commercial lakes are renowned for dropping clear during the winter, and this favours dobbing massively. With such clear water, fish can feed visually, often picking out your bright hook bait as it flutters through the depths.

Dobbing suits both running line and pole tactics but for this one I'm going to cover dobbing on the pole.

Dobbing Bait

White bread is undoubtedly the most famous and popular bait for use when dobbing. Its bright white colour makes it extremely visual in clear water and its soft, fluffy texture allows fish to easily suck it in as it sinks slowly through the water. Despite its soft texture it is surprisingly durable when hooked correctly.

Bread punches are essential here, helping me accurately and easily create a hookbait. A fresh Warburtons Toastie loaf is one of the best for this, as its sticky texture helps it stay on the hook for longer. A 6mm punch is my go-to for ▶

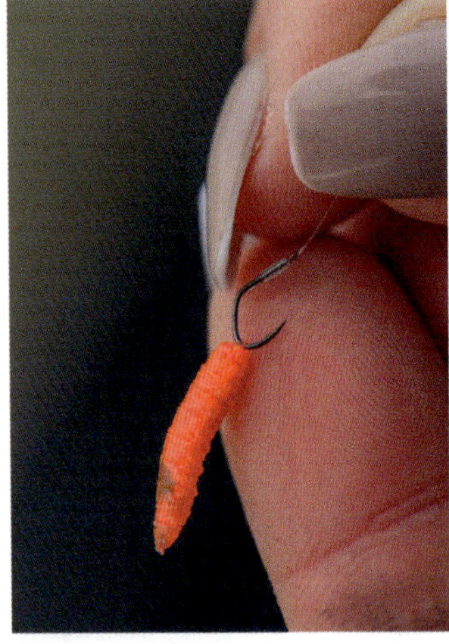

ABOVE LEFT: On days when small fish aren't a problem, a live or dead red maggot can be a brilliant dobbing hookbait.

ABOVE RIGHT: Fjuka Neeonz are always on my side tray when it comes to dobbing. They are really resilient and offer a great hookbait option.

RIGHT: What right thinking carp could resist?

BELOW: A visible bristle is a must when fishing up to cover like reeds, especially when the low winter sun comes out to play.

days when F1s are the predominant target. If some carp are likely to be in on the action too, a 7mm punch is perfect with an 8mm punch in reserve for days when I'm targeting big carp alone. Compressing your bread before hooking will help it stay on the hook as you swing it into position. Make sure you take plenty of bread with you and change your slice once it has dried up. I like to keep mine covered with a bait tub to help protect it from the elements.

> **Make sure you take plenty of bread with you and change your slice once it has dried up. I like to keep mine covered with a bait tub to help protect it from the elements.**

Another bait that I'm going to lump in with bread here is Fjuka - or specifically Fjuka Neeonz. These bright, hookable baits are brilliant for dobbing, and the fact that they come supplied in bright fluorescent colours means you have the option of using bright yellow, pink, or orange baits as well as white.

Another hookbait of choice when dobbing is maggots, a bait which I'm rarely without when fishing commercials during the winter months. At the very least they offer me a change hookbait, but also provide more

visual attraction than bread as they wriggle through the water. I have found great success using maggots for dobbing, especially when the water has a touch more colour than usual which can make bread less effective. It's a simple case of trial and error with hookbaits and the 'best' can be very venue specific.

Location, Location, Location

Dobbing isn't a method for every peg, and despite its negative approach it usually lends itself to pegs with more fish present - after all you can't dob what's not in front of you.

The first thing to look for when it comes to targeting fish are the ones that you can see. As the fish within large shoals of carp and F1s bump into one another they will often start topping and breaking the water's surface. A single topping fish can be the tip of the iceberg, with a much greater number of fish sitting below. A few topping fish is an even better sign of where potential 'dobbers' might

be sat. Remember to take a mental note of exactly where you've seen fish topping because this can give you a valuable head start come the beginning of your session.

If you happen to be sat on a number of 'semi dormant' fish, you are likely to bump into them as you plumb up your other lines, too. Watch out for this as It's a great way of locating groups of fish present in your swim. I will often drag a small plummet around before I start fishing, and once I feel where the fish are sitting, I'll use this as a 'starter for ten' to influence where I start dobbing.

Feature Finder

Features above and below the water's surface play a massive roll in dobbing, helping to hold fish in certain areas of the lake. The most

Be prepared for a mix of sizes when dobbing. Often, fish of different stamps will shoal together, so don't be surprised if one fish is 1lb, and the next is 10lb.

LEFT:
When fishing bread, hook it as centrally as possible. This will mean it stays on the hook for longer.

lake, my minimum depth would be proportionally less, say half of the full depth of the lake for example.

These features often hold what I call 'stragglers' too - so if you are not on one of the main shoals or 'stacks' of dobbers, the chances are that any fish that are in front of you will be sitting tight to cover. Typically, though, if you are on a big shoal of dobbers, you will find them in open water.

This brings me on nicely to slopes, a less obvious feature found beneath the water's surface. Slopes are massively attractive, providing the fish with a sense of safety as they shoal together. On commercial snake lakes the far and near slopes are hugely important. On open water style lakes, the marginal slopes are a brilliant ▶

BELOW:
The cleverest dobbers will always leave themselves somewhere to go for as long as possible - so if the fish back off, you are able to follow them.

obvious features are those which reside above the water. These might include reed beds, bridges, and spinners used to aerate the water in summer. Any structures or vegetation that provide cover are brilliant places to target when

up to a beautifully plump reed bed if It's sitting above just 12in of water. On most venues I'd like to find at least three feet of water under a feature to warrant any time spent fishing to it. On some shallower venues, where 3ft might be the deepest anywhere in the

> **It's very rare that carp and F1s sit dormant on the bottom. In most instances they'll be grouped together mid water at varying depths.**

dobbing, providing a haven for fish often hiding from predators which can easily pick them out through the clear water. When picking a feature to dob against It's important that you check the depth next to it before wasting any time. You have little chance of success fishing

place to target and are often overlooked. Any variations in depth can be crucial when it comes to dobbing so take some time when plumbing up, ensuring you have fully mapped out your peg before the start. Of course, if you start bumping into fish and feel a big shoal is present, put your plummet down and sit patiently for the start of the match - you don't want to push them out of your peg before the all-in.

> ❝ *Ensuring that your hookbait falls slowly through the water plays a big part in dobbing bread successfully.* ❞

Whether you're fishing against a slope or a feature above the surface, fishing at the correct depth is super important. As with all types of pole fishing, nailing your depth can literally make or break a session. It's very rare that carp and F1s sit dormant on the bottom. In most instances they'll be grouped together mid water at varying depths. For that reason, to start a session dobbing, I will typically set my rig around a foot off the bottom and then adjust accordingly. As when shallow fishing for F1s, you can use liners and indications to help find the perfect depth. If you miss an odd bite or are unfortunate enough to foul hook a fish, It's a sure sign that you're fishing too deep. On the other hand, a complete lack of indications is either a sign that you're fishing too shallow or there are simply no fish present in those areas. An adjustment of just a few inches can be enough to kick start a day to remember.

How Shallow!?

Despite the best depth for dobbing usually being between two and four feet below the water's surface, on some days the fish will sit far shallower than you might expect. I have seen days where huge balls of carp and F1s have sat literally a foot below the surface, basking in some warm winter sun. On these occasions you might have no idea

they're there at all so don't be afraid of changing depths and locations until your luck changes.

The Dobbing Rig

Like every method covered so far in this handbook, terminal tackle plays a big part in your success. When hooking into a fish, I want to generate as little disturbance as possible so as not to spook any remaining carp and F1s. These fish will be on high alert, so a finessed approach is everything. To ensure a smooth exit, a soft elastic is vital, preventing any splashing or panic when near the remaining fish. For F1s, a soft hollow elastic like a yellow Hydro or No8 Preston Dura Hollo running through a long kit is ideal, ensuring plenty of elastic is on hand for the job.

There are a few key qualities which I look for when choosing a float for dobbing. The first is a thick hollow bristle. Bites when dobbing are quite the opposite of most in winter, with lightning-fast 'Houdini' bites very common. A thick bristle is also important to support heavy hook baits like bread, particularly when they take on water and swell. I also like a wire stem for dobbing bread, proving stability and instant cocking of the float, a quality which is vitally important when watching for indications on the drop. My mainline will be 0.15mm and a hooklength diameter between 0.10mm and 0.13mm will be used depending on the fish I'm targeting and the proximity of potential snags.

Ensuring that your hookbait falls slowly through the water plays a big part in dobbing bread successfully. Any dormant fish are likely to watch your bait fall to your chosen depth before moving in for a closer inspection. If your bait was to fall too quickly, they're far less likely to show any interest at all. To gain the desired effect I'll place just two number 12 Stotz down my line, spaced equally apart with the remaining shot directly under the float.

A big hook is crucial when dobbing, there's no place for a size 20 here! I use a size 16 Guru F1 pellet hook, offering a medium wire for finesse and a wide gape for accepting larger hook baits like bread. This hook may sound far too big for the winter months but once your bread has swollen up, your size 16 will be nowhere to be seen. If single maggot is my hook bait of choice, I'll scale down to an 18 to help mask the hook.

ABOVE:
Big punches for bigger carp, small punches for F1s.

BELOW:
A lovely mirror on the bread.

LEFT:
A short float with a nice, visible hollow bristle for dobbing.

The Fishing

Dobbing is a great way of starting a session during the cooler months. It presents a chance to watch anglers around you and gives you time to plan your next move. By dobbing you aren't introducing any bait into your peg, avoiding any detrimental effect on the remainder of your session. If you go all guns blazing with maggots and pellets, and the fish aren't feeding, you run the risk of pushing them out of your peg.

When dobbing, patience couldn't be any more important. The last thing that you want to do is push the bulk of fish out of your peg before having the chance to reap maximum rewards. To ensure you get the best from your peg always start dobbing as close as you dare. I'm not by any means suggesting that you should start dobbing on a top kit, but if I haven't seen or found any fish when plumbing up, I will start at a reasonable distance out,

RIGHT:
A lovely net of winter carp.

BELOW:
A Guru F1 pellet hook is a nice light pattern for mixed dobbing work, which will help your bait fall slowly through the water. I would step up to a Super LWG or stronger if bigger fish were on the cards though.

say 11 or 13 metres, and give myself the chance to chase the fish as they slowly move out of range. Quite often, I'll start straight in front of me and work left or right in 6in intervals until I get my first indication or bite. Once you find a group of fish, spend some time in those areas before moving ever so slightly further. The shoal of fish will inevitably move out of reach but by pressing carefully you can catch more before they do. The last thing you want to do is catch one and then move a metre to the left, likely to be right among the shoal of fish. The next fish will probably be your last. Build a mental picture of the fish in front of you and select

> **66** *On red-letter days, you can quite literally spend all day catching dobbing, often putting together a winter weight you'll never forget.* **99**

them one by one from the edges of the shoal.

On red-letter days, you can quite literally spend all day catching dobbing, often putting together a winter weight you'll never forget. For the most part however, dobbing can be great when looking to pick up a bonus carp or a few F1s before they move out of reach. Pay close attention to the anglers around you because if they're catching by feeding bait, It's likely that dobbing isn't the right method on the day. By the same token, if no one is catching anything I would happily spend the first few hours dobbing bread in the hope of catching a few feeding fish later in the session. ■

SOFT PELLET SUCCESS

While water temperatures remain low, the appeal of soft pellets is sure to tip the odds in your favour when carp, F1s and skimmers are the target.

During the cooler months I find soft pellets to be particularly important. The reason for their effectiveness is simple, their soft and fluffy texture makes them far more palatable to any feeding fish. As water temperatures drop, cold-blooded fish feed far less as they're simply much less active. With a lower density than the hard pellets you'd normally feed in summer, soft pellets are much easier to digest so carry a far stronger appeal to both carp and F1s.

BELOW:
Soft pellets are among the deadliest approaches for big bags of carp and F1s in the colder months.

I'll refer to soft pellets throughout this handbook as their versatile texture makes them important to a range of different methods. For this section, I'm going to focus specifically on pole fishing for carp and F1s.

Bait Choice

As I have already touched on, it's the nature of soft pellets which makes them so effective. For that reason, correct preparation is highly important. In terms of feed bait, without doubt 2mm, or 'micro' pellets are my go-to. Where I have a choice, i.e., on venues that don't insist on the use of 'fishery own' pellets, I'll always choose a Skrettings version. With a lower oil content than many they will absorb more water becoming fluffier and fall through the water more slowly, two factors which play a big part in their attraction. When it comes to preparation, there really aren't any hard and fast rules. Every batch of pellets is different so it's important to bear that in mind when soaking them up.

Bear in mind that the end game here is somewhat different to when preparing pellets for feeder fishing. Since a specific texture isn't required to grip around a feeder, it is far easier to soak up micro pellets when pole fishing. You're looking for an entirely soft micro pellet which remains in a uniform pellet shape without sticking to those surrounding it. I usually test a batch at home before soaking on the bank or at least speak to someone who has used them before to give me a rough idea. A bait strainer is essential to ensure that all your pellets are soaked equally. Once drained I tip them into a big bucket to allow them to fluff up uniformly. Where allowed, I will then add a sprinkling of red, yellow, and white Fjuka micros - to add a bit of colour and give another hookbait option.

With feed bait covered, let's talk hookbaits. expander pellets are my go-to in this instance, helping to match the soft nature of my feed pellets. expander pellets are available in a whole host of sizes, but I like to use 2mm and 4mm expanders during the winter months, to cover different scenarios. To prepare them, pour your desired quantity into a small plastic freezer bag and cover them in an equal volume of water. Tie a knot tight to the pellets and leave them in a fridge overnight. By morning they'll be perfect. I keep mine in a tub of water throughout the day to ensure they stay fresh. Don't be alarmed when they all float. The weight of your hook will be enough to sink them.

In the real depths of winter, a 2mm expander, or a Fjuka 3mm hookable micro are my go-to, blending in with my loose fed micro pellets. These are also fantastic when a weight predominantly made up of skimmers is the target. In most other situations I'll choose a 4mm expander. Swapping from a 4mm to a 2mm hookbait, when bites dry up, is a great way of nailing a few extra fish though.

Where to Fish and Feeding

How I feed my micro pellets is largely determined by both the depth of water I'm faced with, and the response from the fish as the session progresses. I always start off fairly negatively in terms of feeding.

On snake lakes, the near and far slopes are brilliant places to target giving you a range of depths to choose from. As a rule, 3ft is a great starting depth allowing you to read the fishes response and plan your ▶

ABOVE:
The RW Dink floats are perfect for this kind of work. Note the wire stem for stability.

BELOW:
F1 Pellet hooks. Fine for finesse, but also super strong.

INSET:
Note the rounded shape, which fits the barrel of the pellet perfectly.

introducing your bait. The first and most common is sprinkling. This involves using a pole pot with a few small holes in, allowing you to tap in a limited number of pellets when required. This way of feeding provides the most attraction as a long column of bait is produced, as well as a bit of (positive) disturbance for the fish to home in on.

The next is what is commonly referred to as 'clumping'. When clumping my pellets, I'll fill my pole pot and gently use my thumb to press them in. Once over my fishing position, I'll slowly dip my pot under the water, allowing the pellets to fall to the bottom in one 'clump'. This method carries far less attraction as the bait falls together, vastly reducing the column of bait created.

The third most common way of feeding micros is in a small ball, important when targeting deeper water. This achieves a similar presentation to the clumping method but will carry your pellets together for longer as they pass through the water column. If I'm fishing in water deeper than 3ft I'll introduce my pellets in this way instead of clumping. Choose the size of your ball dependent on the fish you're targeting and the conditions. If you're after smaller F1s in cooler conditions a ball the size of a pea might be perfect. Whereas if bigger carp are the target you might want to feed a ball the size of a 50 pence piece. Try and match your feeding to the conditions, target species and the response from the fish on the day - but always start off negatively. The biggest single mistake anglers make when it comes to soft pellet fishing is killing their peg via overfeeding.

next move. On prolific days, when fish are actively competing for the falling bait, moving into shallower water will help nail cleaner bites and reduce foul hookers. When fishing with soft pellets all my feeding is carried out via a pole mounted pot. Again, the Guru pole pots are my go-to, this time choosing between a small or medium. The small size is great in the real depths of winter when minimal bait is required, and overfeeding could be extremely damaging. As water temperatures creep up, and more bait is required to generate a response, the medium pot with a sprinkle lid allows me to feed two or three times before having to ship back and refuel.

Whether you're fishing on a sloping snake lake or a big open water, there are a few key ways of

> **66 As water temperatures drop, fish feed far less as they're simply much less active. 99**

For this example, let's say it's mid-February with temperatures just above freezing overnight and I'm fishing a standard commercial snake lake. I'd likely begin my match fishing across to the far bank in around 3ft of water. My small Guru pole pot with the sprinkle lid would be filled with loose, soft 2mm pellets and I'd start by sprinkling in 10 to 15 micros over my fishing position. I'll continue sprinkling every few minutes until I get a response and I'll stick with this feeding pattern until something changes. If I begin to miss bites and foul hook fish, I have two options: either change my feeding or try in shallower water.

Since sprinkling offers so much attraction, I'd first like to alter my depth. Where I'm fishing on a slope my first move would be to grab my

ABOVE:
Some of the Guru pole pots are supplied with the sprinkle lids.

ABOVE RIGHT:
Fjuka Micros can make a great alternative hookbait to an expander on trickier days.

LEFT:
When looking to sprinkle, be careful not to overfill your pot, as this can lead to the bait getting stuck and not releasing properly.

plummet and find some slightly shallower water. Around 2.5ft would be my next go to. If that doesn't work, I'll change from sprinkling to clumping to reduce attraction and pin any feeding fish that are in the vicinity to the bottom. In open water situations where you don't have a slope to work with, changing between sprinkling, clumping and potting balls of micros is the only way of controlling your peg.

A Secret Edge

Groundbait isn't always associated with winter F1 and carp fishing but when it comes to fishing soft pellets, I would never be without a tub of crushed expander pellets, where allowed. I like to think of crushed expanders as an impact bait, helping me draw fish into my swim when times are hard. Feeding it every go is likely to draw fish up off the bottom, but when fed at the right times it can be deadly. Generally, I'll introduce a small ball when bites dry up and I want to draw some fish back into the area. It won't get to the bottom but will leave a trail of scent through the water above my awaiting hookbait, pulling fish in.

RIGHT:
Adding a tape or Tippex mark to your pole will help you be super accurate when fishing up to features.

Be Positive

Using the correct terminal tackle is vital when fishing with soft pellets. Starting at the business end, my hook pattern of choice is always an F1 pellet hook from Tackle Guru. Their wide gape is perfect for rolling an expander onto the hook and its fine wire is strong enough to land bonus carp yet subtle enough to trick timidly feeding F1s and skimmers. If bigger carp are the target, I'd step up to a Super LWG hook, again

> **66** *Every batch of pellets is different so it's important to bear that in mind when soaking them up.* **99**

from Guru. A size 20 F1 Pellet is perfect when 2mm expanders are being used while an 18 or 16 would be my choice when using a 4mm. When the fishing is prolific a 16 will be employed. Preparation is a must here giving you the choice to change when required. Mainline will be 0.15mm, something nice and durable but not thick enough to catch the wind and pull my rig out of position on windy days. My hooklength diameter again depends on each situation but 0.09mm is my standard, ▶

Balanced kit is a must on soft pellets, as bigger fish can show at any time.

> ❝ *Ideally, you want the fish to swim out of your peg once hooked without causing any disturbance.* ❞

generally delicate. With that in mind a short hook length, with a shot close to your hook, is essential. I'll always start with a four inch version, but I will happily place my final shot as close as two inches away from my hook (placed on my hooklength) if missed bites become an issue. For this same

BELOW:
Get set up so you can ship back smoothly, this will help with playing fish and prevent any bait from bouncing out of your pot while shipping out.

> ❝ *This way of feeding provides the most attraction as a long column of bait is produced, as well as a bit of (positive) disturbance.* ❞

with 0.11mm in reserve if bites are plentiful. Elastic choice depends on the time of year and target species. A light hollow elastic is usually my go-to, though I will drop down to a light solid if skimmers are the predominant species in shallow water. Ideally, you want the fish to swim out of your peg once hooked without causing any disturbance.

One thing to keep in mind when using soft pellets is that bites are

INFLUENCER

Some years ago, I remember drawing a peg at Heronbrook, and asking Jamie Hughes for advice on how to fish it. "Should I line up with that tree over there?" I remember asking him. He looked at me in shock. "Try lining up with that blade of grass." He said, pointing at a small piece hanging in the water. This was when I realised the level to which he has refined commercial fishing in terms of accuracy and presentation.

It's a lesson I haven't forgotten and one that will serve you well, when it comes to accuracy in feeding and presentation, look after the inches and the feet will follow. Jamie is a true inspiration, and in terms of cash won, the most successful match angler of all time.

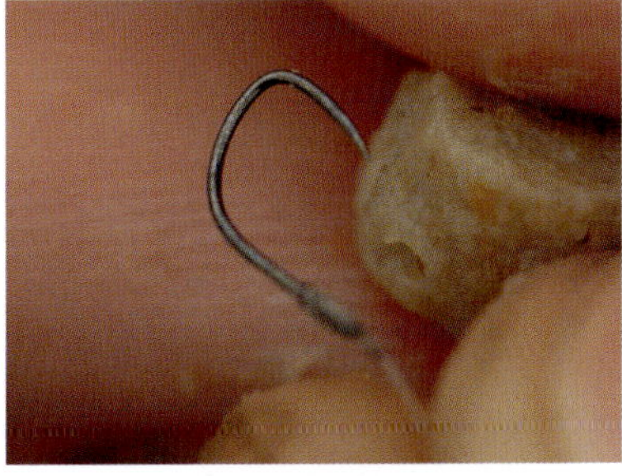

consisting of two No8 shot around four inches from my float. This will help keep the float still, while allowing you to lift at any small indications. While I'm on this topic it's worth mentioning that striking like Zorro is a big no-no. A forceful strike will lead to your soft expander coming off the hook, forcing you to ship back to rebait. A small lift is all that is required to set the hook.

And a final word on soft pellets. As you can tell, the feeding with this bait is very negative compared to a lot of other winter methods. For this reason, it needs space, and water to work. If you were to try and fish pellets next to a positive groundbait line, for example, the danger might be that you 'split your fish', and neither method would prove effective. I have had my best successes on pellets when I have committed to fishing them almost exclusively - or at least fished them in an area of my peg where there isn't a lot else happening. This way, you are giving the negative feeding required the best chance of proving effective. ∎

reason, a positive shotting pattern is a must. Unlike most of my other winter fishing, where small No10 and No11 shot are in action, with soft pellets I only use No9s. I like to have my first shot above my hooklength knot and the remaining number No9s spread out equally above in a slightly tapered fashion. The better the fishing is, the closer my shots will be together. In all instances my shots will be in the final third of the rig.

> **If you're to catch fish on this method your pellet hookbait must sit completely still on the lake bed.**

stem to hold my float in position. I like to use the RW Dink floats, featuring a wire stem, slim body to cut through any tow and a thin - 1.5mm diameter - hollow bristle. The size of your float must be tailored to the depth of water and the prevailing conditions. In shallower water (three to 5ft) a 4x12 or 4x14 will be my choice while a 4x16 is better suited to deeper water above five feet.

Back shots are my second tool for maintaining stability, usually

Keep it Still

Maintaining complete stability plays a massive role in soft pellet success. If you're to catch fish on this method your pellet hookbait must sit completely still on the lake bed. Of course, in harsh conditions this can be difficult but there are a few things which can help put the odds in your favour. A wire stemmed float is a must, offering more weight in the

TURNING SILVER INTO GOLD

Commercial silverfish fishing has been one of the growth areas in winter match fishing over recent years, and it's easy to see why.

The float dips and shudders slightly, before sliding away. Whallop! A firm strike sees yards of blue elastic streaming out into the lake, as a big brown bream makes its bid for freedom. There really is nothing finer on a cold winter day than catching a big net of hard fighting silvers. With the carp often sitting dormant in winter, it's easy to see why this busy style of fishing is gaining popularity.

As with carp and F1 fishing, there are now some big-money qualifiers to get your teeth into on the commercial silverfish circuit, as well as leagues up and down the country - many of which boast really good numbers.

In this chapter, I am going to talk about fishing with natural baits and groundbait. Keep in mind that pellets can also be a deadly bait for commercial skimmers though, and often a combined approach with some groundbait lines (covered here) and a pellet line (covered on pages 84-89) can be the way to go.

When you look at 30lb of silvers in a weigh sling it looks an impressive net of fish. Straight away, thoughts of piling in groundbait, and firing in casters everywhere come to the forefront of the mind... but often this is one of the worst things that you can do.

Like their golden cousins, commercial silvers are cuter than ever - and its only by refining your approach that you can hope to be successful. In a nutshell, if you are hoping to take lessons from natural water bream fishing and apply it to commercials, think again.

Less is More

Commercial skimmers in particular can be a nightmare to catch if there is too much bait in your peg. Often,

ABOVE:
Baits like joker and worm are deadly silverfish attractors. They are the key to big weights, but use with caution, as too much of either can ruin a peg.

LEFT:
Commercial silverfish fishing has been one of the fastest growing areas of the sport in recent years.

BELOW:
Accuracy is crucial when feeding small amounts of bait for big weights of fish. Make sure you know exactly where your bait is going in relation to your pole tip.

I will feed a 'positive' line (with three balls or cups of bait) and a negative line with just a golf ball sized nugget - and on several occasions I have caught good skimmers over the small pile of bait, and smaller fish - or sometimes no fish - on the positive line.

There are of course days when the fish do want to have a feed, and then the positive line comes into its own. But always give yourself a negative option!

There are a couple of reasons why this happens. When the fishing is good, a lot of fish feeding on a silty bottom (which it invariably is on commercial fisheries) will lead to the bottom being stirred up, and it's difficult to attain good bait presentation.

When the fishing is not so good, you need to create competition - so by having less bait on the bottom in an area, the fish are more likely to go down and snaffle it before one of their mates does!

There is one caveat to this philosophy though. The short ▶

> 66 *Piling in groundbait, and firing in casters everywhere come to the forefront of the mind... but often this is one of the worst things that you can do.* 99

ABOVE:
Preston Innovations' No5 elastic is a firm favourite when it comes to mixed nets of winter silvers.

pole line! Here, you can often find a nice firm bottom, so you can afford to be more positive. This line really comes into its own in two scenarios. Firstly, if there are a lot of small fish to catch, and it turns into a 'roach day'. When this happens, you are looking to catch large numbers of fish, so having some bait in your peg is an advantage.

The other situation might be that you are looking to catch the odd bigger fish on this swim late in the day. Again, when this happens, you are best having some bait in the peg for the fish to find and congregate over throughout the session.

Playing the Joker

Where bloodworm and joker are allowed, feeding joker is essential, there literally is no better bait for holding fish in your peg. Where

not allowed, I substitute joker for finely chopped worm, and to be honest, treat the two baits very similarly.

When it comes to groundbait, it has to be sweet fishmeal. I love the Blakes Commercial Pole Mix, Sonubaits F1 Dark and Thatchers, and Dynamite Black Swim Stim. I often find a mix between these three that I am happy with at a given venue. Even for roach, in the coldest weather, you will often find a fishmeal mix outscores a sweet one on commercial fisheries. I think it's because the roach get used to high levels of fishmeal

> ❝ *When the fishing is good, a lot of fish feeding on a silty bottom will lead to the lake bed being stirred up, and it's difficult to attain good bait presentation.* ❞

feed throughout the year and their 'normal' diet adapts.

When I'm fishing with joker, leam is also added, often at a 30-50% ratio to the groundbait,

RIGHT:
If the right stamp fish respond to loosefeed, you are on to a winner.

A great tip in low winter light is to incorporate a Stotz, or small shot directly above the eye of your float. If you struggle to see the bristle at any point you can simply slide this small weight up the line.

Slow the Release

The first thing to bear in mind is that both joker and finely minced worm are incredibly potent baits. If fish are in the area, they will eat these offerings enthusiastically and stay in your peg until every last bit is gone. They will scour out the bottom looking for them, and they can become so preoccupied with them that in fact it works against you.

Have too much of these baits in your peg, and you can have a swim full of fish, with bubbles everywhere, line bites… but your only reward is the odd foul hooked fish.

Simple, you might think, just pot bait in little and often. However, it is also sometimes the case that the fish don't respond well to topping up. I've seen plenty of occasions when a single top up ball can kill a swim for the rest of the session, and at best, it often needs a little rest before you can catch fish from the line again.

So, what is the answer? The first feeding strategy that I often use, predominantly on the short line is locking bait in your balls! When mixed on the damp side, the right groundbait allows you to trap the 'loose' offerings tight within the balls of groundbait. Leam helps here when fishing with joker, as you can really squeeze the balls tightly so they break down slowly.

When fishing with worms, it's more a case of adding the chopped worm to your mix until it forms a stiff stodge, that sinks as one and breaks down

slowly. The effect you are looking for is a steady stream of active bait being exposed in your peg - but never too much, too quickly.

This strategy doesn't work so well on a soft bottom though. Why? It's back to the silt problem. Hard squeezed balls tend to sink into silt, which creates a range of problems. So, we have to apply different thinking.

My preference is to feed some joker or worm in groundbait at the start as a primer, then loose feed bait regularly, and get the fish feeding on the drop. Bringing fish off the bottom

> **66** *Even for roach, in the coldest weather, you will often find a fishmeal mix outscores a sweet one on commercial fisheries.* **99**

is a perfect way to negate the silt problem, you get nice clean bites and can catch really efficiently. If you can catch the right stamp of fish by loose feeding, you are in a great position.

That said, the fish don't always like to feed like this. On some days, loosefeed is detrimental, so it's not just a case of going in all guns blazing. I think it far safer to loosefeed a little on one of the long lines, and gauge the response. If ▶

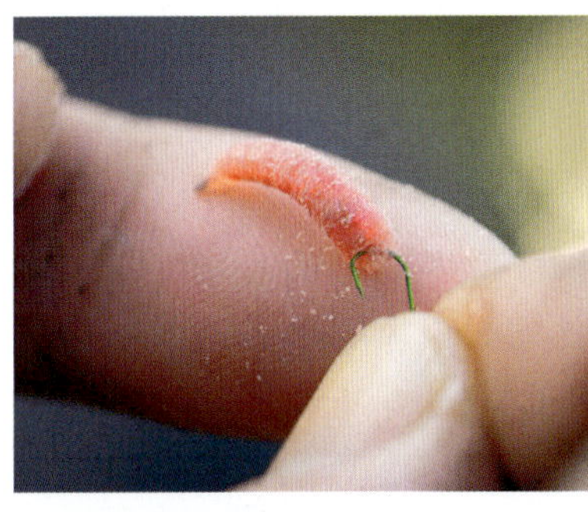

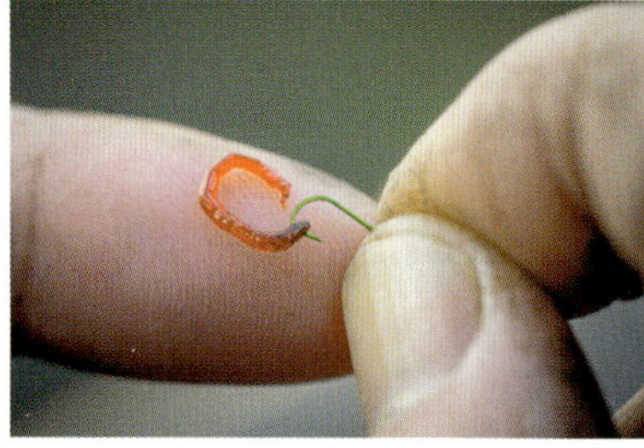

ABOVE: In the hardest conditions, there is rarely a better bait than single bloodworm - but when its milder, you often find maggot and caster will sort out the bigger fish.

ABOVE:
It's often worth loosefeeding on a short pole line, to group fish for a late extraction!

they come to it - happy days, if they don't then a different approach is needed.

At times, 'decking it'- presenting a bunch of bloodworm or a small redworm or dendrobaena hookbait hard on the bottom - can be deadly way of catching fish. Its effectiveness can be limited on silty venues though, as topping up with groundbait as we have previously mentioned can lead to a whole world of pain, so you have no real way of feeding to keep the fish in the area.

Often the best way round this problem is to take your initial fish from the line, and when it starts to peter out, top up with small, marble sized balls of raw joker or worm. Because it is light, this tends to sit on top of the silt, and can give your peg another lease of life.

Rigs

I have described two very different ways of catching fish.

Decking a bait on the bottom and presenting a falling bait to catch fish in among your loosefeed. Essentially, I like to set up a rig for each of these two jobs - the strung rig for a falling bait is a 4X14 old style Preston Chianti float, with No11 shot spread down the lower third of the rig.

The deck rig is a 0.5g Rive Series 6, with a bulk of No9s 14in from the hook and two No9 droppers.

I actually don't think the specific floats that you choose to use are that important. As long as you understand how the gear that you are using works in the water, and

can dot floats down for sensitivity where required. Crucially, you must also be sure that you can see the bristle in the low winter light.

One thing that is a constant when it comes to winter silvers though is small hooks, light lines and light elastics. The Gamakatsu greens are a firm favourite for both bloodworm and maggots and casters, with a Guru F1 pellet in

> **66** *The effect you are looking for is a steady stream of active bait being exposed in your peg - but never too much, too quickly.* **99**

a size 18 being a slightly beefed up alternative on good days. The Preston No5 Slip elastic is a wonderful shock absorber for mixed silverfish, and a firm favourite, scaling down to No4 on shallower water, or if the skimmers are smaller, or stepping up to a No6 in deeper water, or if bigger fish regularly feature.

Reading back through this chapter, I can understand why anglers might be confused by successful silverfish targeting on commercial fisheries. As you can tell, 90% of the art lies in the

Winter commercial silverfish fishing is rarely about numbers. Catch the right stamp of fish, and you are onto a winner.

feeding. I have outlined a lot of scenarios, but hopefully I have got you thinking along the right lines.

The biggest single mistake anglers make on commercial silverfish matches is overfeeding. Too many anglers see the guy next to them catching and decide to pot a load of bait in, killing any chance they have of a comeback.

> **" I can understand why anglers might be confused by successful silverfish targeting on commercial fisheries. As you can tell, 90% of the art lies in the feeding. "**

If you can catch loose feeding, you are often on the shortest route to success, as you can feed to your bites, while drawing fresh fish in all the time. On the days when this doesn't work, feeding multiple lines is important, so you can work out how the fish respond to topping up, while keeping options open and feeding your net all day. ■

Giving yourself options is the key to big weights of winter silvers. When it comes to feeding, less generally means more in the net.

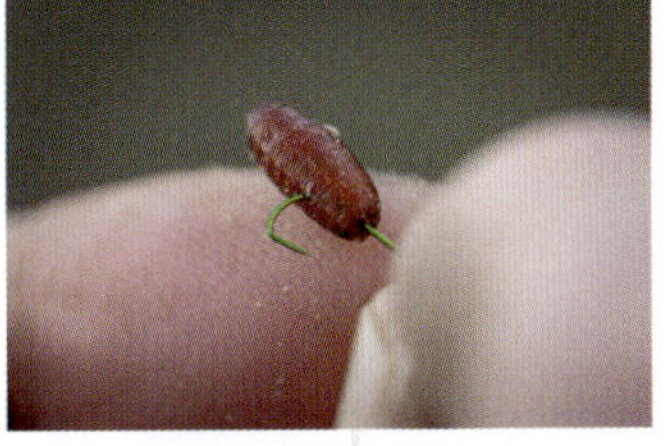

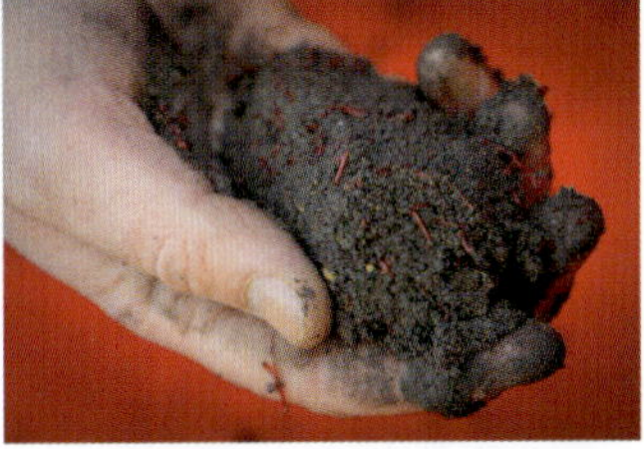

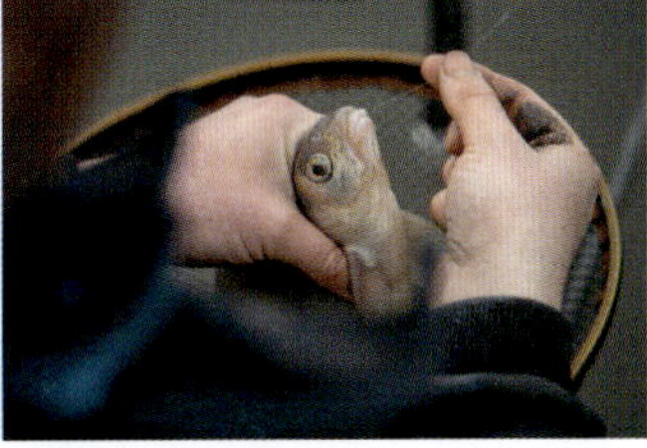

THE
FISH FINDER!

As negative as it may seem, the 'straight lead' or bomb can be the best way to find big fish in winter, without spooking them out of your peg.

East Midlands based John Whincup shows the type of beast that can fall to the straight bomb approach. You don't need many of these for a match win.

On open water lakes where big carp and F1s are the target, the bomb can be among the most useful tools and methods that you have at your own disposal during the winter months. Not only is it a great fish catching method in its own right, but it can also be used to help you find the fish. So, even on days when you don't get a bite on it, it can massively influence how you approach your match.

I'm going to cover two sides to winter bomb fishing here, using the bomb as a way of searching your peg, or 'dobbing' and then examine how you can catch over feed. We will start with the bomb as a tool for 'dobbing' at range.

Tackle first, and there are a couple of important things to mention. Firstly, I think you want a

BELOW:
Light bombs and fine tips mean you spook less fish.

nice soft rod for bomb fishing in the winter. You need to be able to read your bites and liners, and the use of a soft tip helps you to do this. I love the Shimano Aero X7 rods for this kind of work, as they actually feature a spliced 3/4 oz tip, which is super sensitive. Other great rods are available, just make sure they have a nice, light tip. Using these, on a fairly slack line, I am able to pick up subtle liners without spooking fish - as you sometimes do when fishing with a heavier tip that requires a heavier bomb.

Unless you are fishing up to snags, a light mainline is also an advantage. I use 6lb Guru Dragline

Often, you aren't looking for many bites in winter - so being patient brings its rewards.

for a lot of this sort of work. Super strong, but also easily castable and a line that performs very well in the wind. In terms of my setup, the rig is identical to the one I use in summer. So, where it's allowed I use a simple swivel and clip running on the line, down to a loop housing the clip from a Guru waggler adapter. Where this setup is not allowed, I simply have a running bomb down to a leger stop.

Find the Fish

Before I go into how I find and catch the fish, I want to make a couple of points about watercraft. These may sound extreme, but years of experience tell me that they hold true. Once the water temperature drops below a certain point, the fish have little interest in feeding, and as such there is little incentive for them to come in towards the bank. Visit most commercials in winter and you tend to find the best pegs are at the biggest, widest part of the lake for this reason. These are the pegs where the fish can get as far

away from bankside disturbance as possible.

So, keeping that idea in mind - that the fish are constantly trying to get away from disturbance - you need to think about every aspect of your approach. On tightly pegged venues, you might notice that some top anglers are the last to get to their pegs. This is because they believe that the commotion of everyone else setting up will push fish into their areas. Other top anglers might

> **❝ On tightly pegged venues, you might notice that some top anglers are the last to get to their pegs. ❞**

set up quickly, then leave their areas to settle, again, so fish will come in and settle in front of them while

LEFT:
My favoured rig (where allowed) the same as used in summer, and invented by the great Paul Holland.

BELOW:
An inline bomb down to a stop is used where fisheries insist on no knots above the feeder

other anglers are banging around on the bank. For me, the key is to be as quiet as possible, so you minimise the chance of disturbing anything.

It makes me cringe when, during the setup period for example, you see anglers repeatedly casting to the middle of the lake to set their clip, or casting to their limit and leaving their rod in to look for liners. I understand the logic, but the way I see it is every liner you get while not fishing is potentially a fish that you could have spooked without giving yourself the chance of catching it. So, for me, stealth is key whether before the match or when it starts. ▶

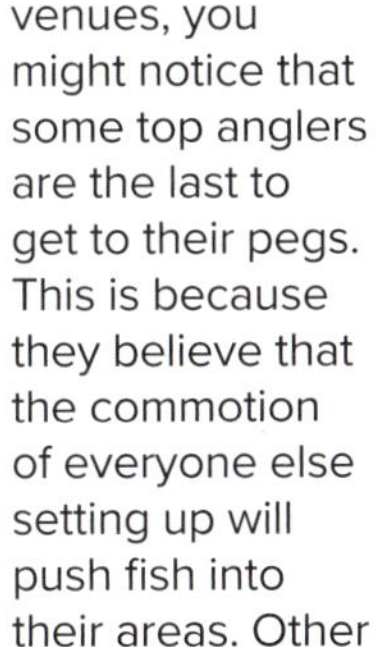

In terms of where I make my first cast, it largely depends on how many bites I am hoping for or expecting. You have to imagine the fish are probably more spread out at the start of the session than they will be a couple of hours in, after they have shoaled up to get away from the pressure of anglers. For example, if you are on a fairly tightly pegged match and have drawn a narrow end of the lake, realistically you might only be looking for a couple of bites before the fish back off to the wider areas - so I'd cast to where I most expected a bite straight away. However, if I had been lucky enough to draw a wide peg, or somewhere where I knew the fish backed off to, I might be more inclined to start closer than my limit, or start on another method, so that the fish back off into my area. Once carp settle in winter, unless you do something

ABOVE:
A soft tip, set fairly slack is best, as it lets you read liners without spooking fish.

RIGHT:
A soft, fine mesh landing net is always used when hair rigs are concerned.

BELOW:
A fish hooked in the bottom lip is a good sign as it means the hook has turned properly into the fishes mouth.

catastrophically wrong, you tend to find you catch them. So if yours is a known peg, or wide area, it can be well worth just sitting back and letting them come to you before trying to catch them.

Bread Winner!

My number one bait for this 'dobbing' style is definitely bread. I find this stuff will bring bites when everything else fails. The only criticism sometimes with it is that it can be difficult to keep on the hook when fishing at distance or when bite times are slower. In recent years, I have found a good way of countering this though. I make what I call a 'Fjuka sandwich'. Literally, this is two bits of bread either side of a squashed white floating Neeonz. The result is a bait that is super buoyant and stays on the hook better than three disks of bread - but retains

> ## " The way I see it is every liner you get while not fishing is potentially a fish that you could have spooked without giving yourself the chance of catching it. "

the lovely, soft, fluffy edges that carp love so much.

Hook wise for bread, it really does depend on the size of fish that I am targeting. For big carp, I might go for a size 10 or 12 Guru QM1. I believe big fish simply suck in bread, and move off, so this is perfect. For smaller fish like F1s, a size 14 or 16 KKM is preferred, as they can fit it in their mouths more easily. In terms of hooklength length, eight inches or 12in is right in most situations.

If bites don't come on bread I will try corn, or a popup as a change bait - but to be honest when dobbing on the bomb, if it doesn't go around on bread, you can be a bit scuppered.

A good, strong catapult helps make sure you corn goes the distance.

LEFT:
Loosefeeding corn doused in Sensate liquid has brought good recent results.

Single corn, mounted on a quickstop is generally my choice of hookbait on the corn line.

BELOW:
I love the Guru Breadboards and punches. Perfect for keeping all your tackle together, and you can close the lid and keep the bread in great nick.

Where to Cast?

After making the first cast, I gauge the response and then plan my next move. If I get little liners, I know I'm in the right area. Big liners tend to suggest the carp are closer to me, and higher up in the water column. If you are on an area that you

expect to improve, it's important not to panic, and to give the swim time to develop. I certainly wouldn't go to the area that I expect to be best in this scenario until I know some fish are feeding. The last thing you want to do is push dormant fish out of your peg before you've had chance to catch a few.

Often on this kind of winter match you are only looking for a handful of bites to do very well, so be considered, take your time, and keep your head straight. It is VERY easy to blow your peg before it's even got going. Keep an eye on what other anglers are doing around the lake, as this will give you a good idea of where the fish are, and what direction they are likely to come from, if they aren't in front of you early. It will also give you an idea of when the fish have switched on to feed, so you can be ready. ▶

It doesn't take many of these to build a match winning weight!

Loosefeed

Up to now, what I have covered is basically dobbing on the rod, searching out fish on a single hookbait. I will almost always combine this approach with loosefeed, so I have somewhere to go in the swim where I have fed some bait. At some point in most matches, you get what's called a 'feeding window', where the fish have a bit of a munch. This is when this line can really come into its own!

66 *If yours is a known peg, or wide area, it can be well worth just sitting back and letting them come to you before trying to catch them.* **99**

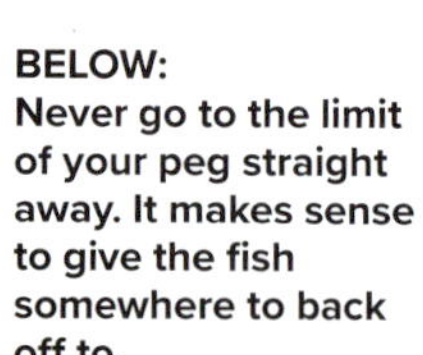

BELOW: Never go to the limit of your peg straight away. It makes sense to give the fish somewhere to back off to.

Guru's QM1 Hooks are the choice when bread, and bigger baits are being used.

When I say loosefeed, the amount I put in is far less than in summer. One tin of corn is loads for most winter sessions. Like Tommy Pickering, I have had some success lately soaking my corn in Sensate liquid, so that it absorbs the flavour. I have caught lots of carp on this, along with a fair few big skimmers, too.

To play it safe, my loosefeed area is always well short of where I am casting without feed - so in effect I have the best of both worlds, an area where the fish can come to feed, and also somewhere where I can catch the fish that have backed away from bait and anglers. It's well worth having a Method feeder set up here, too, as covered in the winter Method feeder chapter. Some days, presenting a little neat pile of bait Method feeder style will

outperform the straight lead on this line - and on other days, the reverse is true.

I tend to loosefeed right from the start of the match with between six and ten pieces of corn every five or ten minutes, but I'm happy to up the ante if the fish respond well.

Depending on where you are fishing and the depth of the lake, liners when you are fishing long will

66 *To be honest, when dobbing on the bomb, if it doesn't go around on bread, you can be a bit scuppered.* **99**

often betray the presence of fish on your shorter, loosefeed line.

In terms of tackle on this line, again it's light bombs and a size 16 or 14 KKM hook to a 12in hooklength. When the fish respond well here, it's worth experimenting with the regularity of your casts, as

Never bully fish, but play fish firmly, and land them as quickly as possible. The last thing you want is fish charging all over your swim and disturbing things.

> **If you are on an area that you expect to improve, it's important not to panic, and to give the swim time to develop.**

often the optimum catch rate can be achieved by casting fairly regularly.

A final point on this swim. When it goes, it's great but I have known plenty of sessions where it doesn't

work too, so never get preoccupied with it. If you don't cast on the line and get regular indications and bites, you are better off on your single bait line.

The Fjuka Floating Neeonz are great when used along with bread. They make it more buoyant and stay on the hook well.

INFLUENCER

Tom Pickering must be credited here. I've been lucky enough to work with him several times shooting content about this sort of fishing.

Observation and patience are two of the biggest edges that Tommy uses. With his trademark flask, and hand on his chin, he will happily wait for things to start happening, while others around him blow their pegs. By reading the water, and watching what is being caught around the lake, he is able to gauge when the fish have switched on to feed and adjust his plan accordingly. The biggest mantra he has taught me is 'let the fish tell you what to do next'. And it's so true. By keeping an open mind and being adaptable you make the best possible decisions.

Hopefully, these few tips will help the next time you are presented with some winter bomb fishing. The trick is not to panic, you may not need many bites to frame. ■

LEFT:
Try dosing your corn in Fjuka's Sensate liquid - it often brings extra bites.

THE CARP TRAP

One rig to catch a big weight of winter carp? It must be the Method feeder.

BELOW:
The Method or hybrid feeder is perfect for catching winter carp, presenting a small, neat pile of bait right where you want it.

f I had to choose one method for a weight of carp when the temperatures drop, for me it's the Method feeder. In an earlier chapter, I explained the effectiveness of a bomb and single hookbait approach - but the big difference with the Method is that it catches fish that *want* to feed - and allows you to build a peg.

As with the chapter on the 'Modern Method' where I focussed on Method feeder fishing in the summer, in this chapter I'm talking about a slightly broader church, covering hybrid feeder, and pellet feeder as well. The common theme is these are all bolt rigs, where you are effectively setting a 'carp trap', with a small pile of bait with a hookbait in it. When a carp sucks in this pile of bait, it hooks itself.

I'm not going to spend too long on rod, line, or feeder size/ weight choice as there is nothing really different to what was covered in the warm weather Method feeder chapter, so if you have any doubts simply revisit that section.

One area of tackle that does bear a mention though is line and hooklength diameter, as often you can get away with finer tackle in the colder months as the fish don't fight as hard. As I have said throughout, fishing light, where you can get away with it, is a big advantage. Lighter mainlines mean you can hold the bottom with lighter feeders, which make less disturbance as they enter the water. Lighter hooklengths, and smaller hooks mean more bites, and fish in the net.

> ❝ **You can get away with finer tackle in the colder months as the fish don't fight as hard.** ❞

As my general rule, 0.13mm diameter Reflo Power is used for 90% of winter hooklengths - but if the fish seem in aggressive mood, I'll go up to 0.15mm or 0.17mm. Mainline-wise, it's down from 8lb in summer to 6lb in winter. Light tips are a must, so 1oz maximum for most work, or scaling down to 3/4 oz if fishing up to islands.

Colour is King

I used to believe that your hookbait really didn't matter on the method feeder, as the fish are generally sucking in the whole pile of bait - but recent experience has definitely made me change my mind -and especially in winter. I have had days over the last couple of years when I can only get

ABOVE:
Perfect micros ready for the feeder. Soft on the outside, but still firm on the inside so they swell up and push off the frame of the feeder.

LEFT:
Pushing your hook into your micros after the first squeeze helps keep it in place while you squeeze on the rest of the pellets.

LEFT:
A hybrid feeder loaded and ready for action.

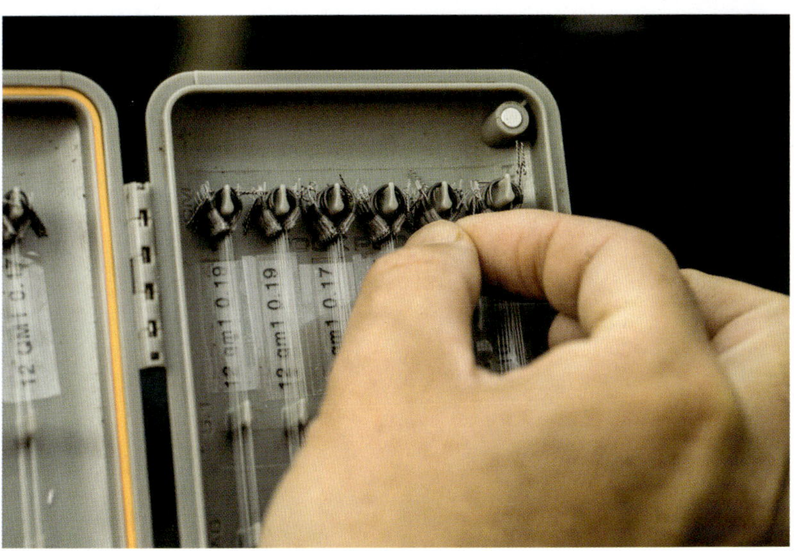

bites on a certain colour hookbait. The invention of wafters has really changed things here. Go in your local shop, and you will see a vast array of these, different shapes, colours, and flavours. Confusingly, talk to a range of top anglers they will often all tell you that they prefer different ones, too.

For me, there are four hook baits that dominate above all else. The Fjuka 6mm wafters (pink or yellow), a 6mm hard pellet (banded) or a single dead red maggot. In the coolest weather, its generally the wafters that score best for me. If you have time for a practice or pleasure session on the venue, this can be time well spent so you can work ▶

LEFT:
Guru QM1s are still a great hook choice, though I'm quick to scale down in terms of line diameters. Doing so definitely brings more bites.

LEFT:
A great hybrid feeder caught carp - held by Tom Pickering, who along with Nick Speed has taught me most of what I know about this kind of fishing.

RIGHT
Hookbait colour can be massive at this time of year, and a pink Fjuka wafter seems to work quite well for me.

BELOW:
Always carry a long landing net pole - when a big fish pops up, you want to be able to reach it.

out what the fish want - then you are sitting confidently come match day.

If you are not catching on a particular day, changing between different colour hook baits can be a worthwhile exercise too. It's amazing how often a subtle change makes a difference, and brings a bite from the blue.

Where to Cast

Fish location is one of the most important aspects of winter fishing. Studying match results will give you a good idea where fish are held up at certain times, and you generally find that these are invariably the same from year to year whenever conditions are comparable. Warm winds, and rising temperatures can make fish move about, but other than this you tend to find that the fish favour the same winter haunts.

Sadly, in match conditions we don't have the option of picking our pegs and sitting in the epicentre, but we can still use watercraft to give ourselves an edge over the competition.

Thinking about where to cast and when to cast there is vital. You have to have a plan for your session, so you always have somewhere to go - and on the toughest days, leaving

> **❝** *I used to believe that your hookbait really didn't matter on the method feeder, as the fish are generally sucking in the whole pile of bait - but recent experience has definitely made me change my mind -and especially in winter.* **❞**

your best area for when you think the fish will feed the best can be the key difference between catching and blanking.

Because when you fish a Method feeder you are feeding bait, I would always avoid throwing to my limit, or where I think the fish may be balled up straight away. I would rather fish near side, and see what response I get. I then have the option of going further towards the fish later, if things don't go well. There is also a risk that if you chuck to your limit straight away and the fish back off, you will lose them.

I like to fish this winter Method approach in conjunction with the

> **66** *Changing between different colour hook baits can be a worthwhile exercise too. It's amazing how often a subtle change makes a difference.* **99**

winter bomb, which I covered in an earlier chapter. This gives me a way of exploring the peg and finding the fish if I need to without feeding bait, and so influences where I chuck my Method feeder when I decide to go in it.

How Long to Leave it

I must admit to being one of the doubters who laughed when I first saw feeder anglers with stopwatches. Overkill, surely! I am now well and truly converted, and it's one of the most useful tools you can have in the winter. It's amazing how often the times that you have to wait between bites are almost identical cast to cast, and once you have spotted this pattern, you can save yourself valuable time by avoiding wasted time in the water.

Denis White had an old saying that the first and the last cast of the day are the most important, and on the hardest day this is definitely true. If you are after just one or two fish, this is when they are most likely to come. The longest I tend to leave any one cast in the water is 20 minutes, and if it's a low weight

day, I'm happy to do this on the first and last cast of the day, to maximise my chance of success.

Of course, if the anglers all around me are playing fish after five minutes, I might well have a recast - it's very much about reading what is going on around you. The other nice thing about a stopwatch is that it allows you to apply a certain mathematical logic to your matches as well. If you are getting a bite every 15 minutes from a 5lb fish, and you think 60lb might be enough to win, you know you can stick to your guns. However, if you think you need 100lb to win and bites are only coming every half an hour from 5lb fish, it's fair to assume you either aren't fishing to win the match, or a change is needed.

ABOVE:
Adding Korda Goo to my Method feeder has bought bites on tricky days.

BELOW:
It doesn't take many of them to build a weight!

BELOW RIGHT:
The Method catches good skimmers, too which are often welcome weight builders on tough days.

Flavourings

Until a few years ago, I never used to use flavourings. But if there is one area when I think they might make a difference, it's winter Method fishing. The truth is, at this time of year, the carp aren't always that keen on eating - so every little edge you can give yourself to generate an extra bite is useful. I have been using Fjuka Sensate for the last 12 months or so, and I definitely think having the flavour in my pellets has bought a few extra fish at times.

I also like the flavourings you can squirt on the feeder to make a cloud in the water, namely the Korda Goo! Smokey Pineapple is probably my favourite, and on those days when you are trying to eke out extra bites from the odd curious fish, this can bring a super quick bite. Use it to make an impact when you cast though, I would rarely be inclined to add it to the feeder every cast.

The Coldest Days

It's worth me talking very briefly about trying to catch carp on the coldest winter days. In these situations, the Method feeder still has its place, but I will almost always use it in conjunction with the bomb. The main reason for this is that I don't want to be emptying bait off the feeder that isn't getting eaten. In the coldest weather, fish might only feed for a very brief window, and when they do feed, having too much bait on the bottom can actually work against you.

With the water cold, the fish don't need much food to survive, so ▶

ready to feed - and crucially a nice clean lake bed with just your feeder and hookbait available.

Even on the toughest of days, it is a mistake to think that the fish will be in the deepest water too by the way. If you have cover, away from disturbance, bites can come when fishing to far bank features, too. Obviously, I wouldn't be casting into inches of water, but it is well worth exploring the bottom of the far ledge, creeping up into the shallower water.

Go Interchangeable

A final point on tackle here. I think the interchangeable stem systems that companies like Guru and Preston make are invaluable at this time of year. With these, you can simply slide off the feeder that you were using, and replace it with a bomb, or vice versa. No need to switch rods, simply change the weight or feeder. This way, you can fish off one clip all day, and give the fish the presentation that they want without needing to interchange rods. ■

their appetites are tempered. I once heard it likened to a human, who might not be very hungry. Offer them half a pig roast, with lashings of fries and they might say no. But a small canape or sweet, and you might get some interest.

So, when the fish switch on to feed, the ideal scenario is you have

> **❝ I must admit to being one of the doubters who laughed when I first saw feeder anglers with stopwatches. Overkill, surely! ❞**

little or no bait on the bottom. On these mega tough days keep your eyes on the anglers around you, and fish with a bomb while ever you don't think the fish are feeding. Then, when they switch on, change to a small Method or hybrid. This literally gives you the perfect presentation in this scenario, a little table loaded with food ready for when the fish are

ABOVE:
The author, with one of Larford Lakes' larger residents, nailed on a hybrid feeder.

RIGHT:
On venues where they are allowed, I will add a sprinkling of Fjuka micros to my normal ones, once soaked. In my mind, this must help the feeder stand out on the bottom.

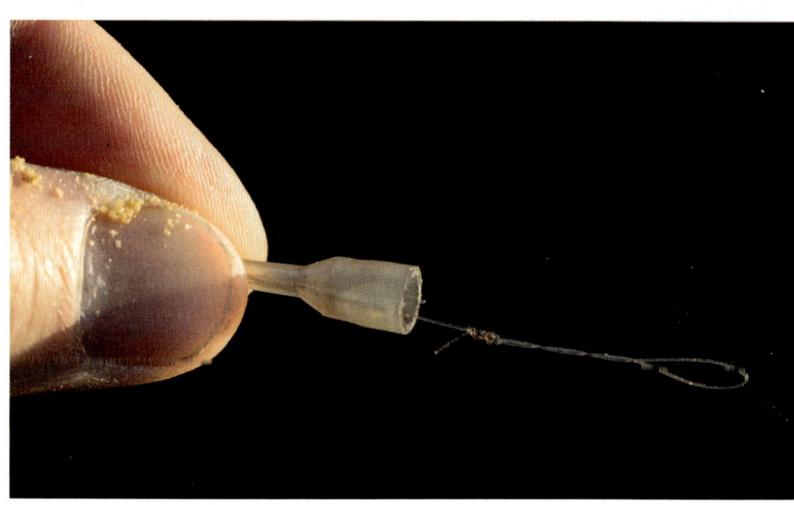

RIGHT:
I do love the Korda and Preston interchangeable feeder systems. They make switching between different feeders (or bombs) a doddle.

Casting to find the fish is vital early on in the session - but don't be surprised if they move into shallower water later.

> **If you are getting a bite every 15 minutes from a 5lb fish, and you think 60lb might be enough to win, you know you can stick to your guns.**

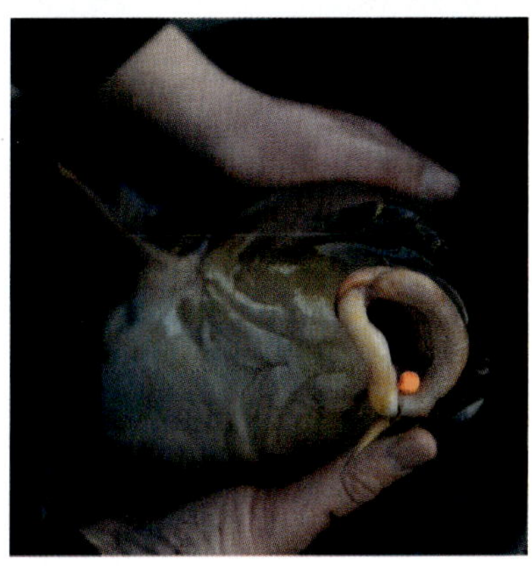

ABOVE:
The neatness of the Method feeder, presenting minimum feed in a compact area make it the ultimate winter carp catcher.

RIGHT:
Carp home in on bright colours in the clearer waters of winter.

INFLUENCER

Nick Speed has massively helped my understanding of this tactic. He has won more matches with carp on rod and line than anyone I know, thanks to his enquiring mind and ability to constantly stay in touch with fish. True pioneers are quite a rare thing in match fishing - but Speedy is one of those people who produces ideas, refines them and turns them into match winners.

PERFECT
PREPARATION

Having the right kit is essential to get you on the road to commercial match fishing success. Here is my guide to what I use and why.

To the angler starting out in match fishing, I hope this handbook has proved a good guide to the key methods you need to win - but for the more experienced angler, I hope you have taken away a good number of tips that can make a difference to your fishing.

This final chapter is all about preparation, and perhaps more than any other part of the book, what I'm covering here is subjective. There really is no right or wrong when it comes to tackle, it's about using what suits your style and the way you like to fish. It's also about what you can realistically afford.

That said, I have certainly found a system that works for me - and hopefully aspects of it can work for you too.

ABOVE:
Buy good quality tackle, look after it, and it will retain some value.

Splash the Cash?

There's no getting away from the fact that match fishing is an expensive sport, and I'm going to start by talking about big items — poles and rods.

True, the prices of some of these are eye-watering, and many match anglers I know spend more on their pole than they do on their family car!

These Nathan Lumb floats are an example of the 'slim' patterns that I mentioned. These are among the strongest that I have found.

spend much of their lives left in the rod bag or lying on the bank.

With rods, it's similar, there are some cracking rods out there for around £100 that will hold their own against even the most expensive rods for most commercial applications.

Big tackle shops often have rod showrooms, and pole alleys now - so you've always got the option to try before you buy. Make sure you take advantage of these, and remember - you don't have to buy the most expensive gear to win matches, but you do need quality kit that's fit for purpose.

Elastics

I'm not going to dwell on elastics for long as there are lots of good ones out there, and a lot depends on the stamp of fish you are catching. Daiwa Hydrolastic, and Preston Hollo or Hybrid elastic is my choice for carp or F1s and lighter, solid Slip elastics come in to play for silvers.

One thing I would like to mention though is a few little details in elastic setup that I think make a difference. The first is Preston Roller Pullas. These are fantastic, and I have them fitted on all my Daiwa top kits. They are really smooth and easy to use, but also help your elastics last longer by reducing friction. ▶

And, there is definitely an element of truth in the saying that you get what you pay for, but the fact is that the big brands do not make bad tackle.

That said, there are two saving graces to spending a few quid on your tackle. The first is that quality gear from respected brands will hold a decent second hand value, as long as you take good care of it, so it's not money lost.

The second saving grace is that to get good quality kit, you tend to only have to go mid-range, what you pay for with the most expensive tackle is tiny incremental gains, which although useful, aren't essential to an angler's every day fishing.

Let me give a couple of examples, firstly poles. If you go to your local pole alley and compare a £1,500 pole with a £5,000 pole you will notice little difference up to say, 13 metres. The more expensive pole might be a bit better, marginally stiffer, marginally lighter, possibly with a slightly slimmer diameter, but the cheaper pole will more than hold its own at the shorter lengths. It's when you add on sections, and start getting out towards 16 metres that the more expensive pole will really come into its own - but you will probably find that the cheaper pole is still very usable. And more than that, it's worth considering how often you actually need a 16 metre pole. Having the option of going to 16 metres can occasionally be an advantage, but the truth is, the extensions that create much of that advantage will

> **66** *You get what you pay for, but the fact is that the big brands do not make bad tackle.* **99**

My three favoured shallow patterns. The two small RW floats for fishing up in the water in feed, and the big MW Cookies for mugging.

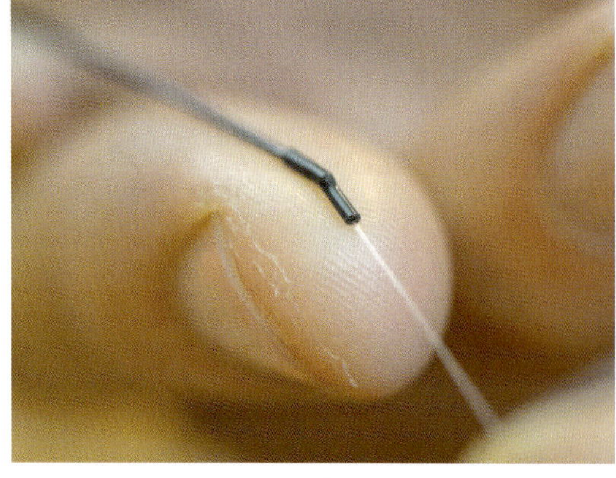

Next up is bushes - it's well worth paying extra for a proper, pure PTFE bush. Daiwa supply these, or you can buy them online, but they work so much better than cheaper plastic types.

Finally, the way you connect your elastic to your line. I have tried lots of different methods over the years, and I definitely think there is an advantage in using the most direct connections possible. I use what I call the Andy Bennett method on most elastics, which is a simple Drennan Swivel Connector bead, with the open end running down to a knot. I then use a simple slip knot in the line behind this knot and slide the bead down to it.

For solid elastics or thicker hollow elastics, I use a simple crows foot connection. Again, direct, light, and simple.

Rigs

Some of the best anglers I know carry hundreds of rigs, all ready to go on winders. Others, who are equally devastating, tie most of their rigs on the bank! The key for me is a happy medium- I like to be prepared but will also try to read the water and be adaptable too. One key principle that is often overlooked is that you have to use what is right on a particular day.

This may sound simple, but I have known plenty of anglers over the years who 'make do'. So they might have tied up rigs which they set up, thinking they are prepared... but not one of the rigs they have tied is quite right. They would have been better off looking at the water, the wind and thinking how they want to fish and then tying up a rig to suit. Use rigs to suit the peg, don't try and force the rigs that you have ready to work if they aren't quite right.

> **"** *For solid elastics or thicker hollow elastics, I use a simple crows foot connection. Again, direct, light, and simple.* **"**

The other big point I want to get across relates to using the tackle that's right for you and learning to read it. Take floats for example, as you will see from the images throughout this handbook I have certain patterns that I swear by, and know how they behave, so I can use them to read the water. In winter, or when the fishing isn't too taxing on my lines, I will happily use the same rig across multiple sessions, too. There is literally no point in stripping them down and remaking them for the sake of it.

I will write briefly about the floats that I use for each style of commercial fishing, but again I stress that these are personal choices, similar patterns from other makers will generally work equally well if you prefer them.

Floats

My go-to float for catching fish on the bottom on pellets, maggots or meat is what I am going to call a

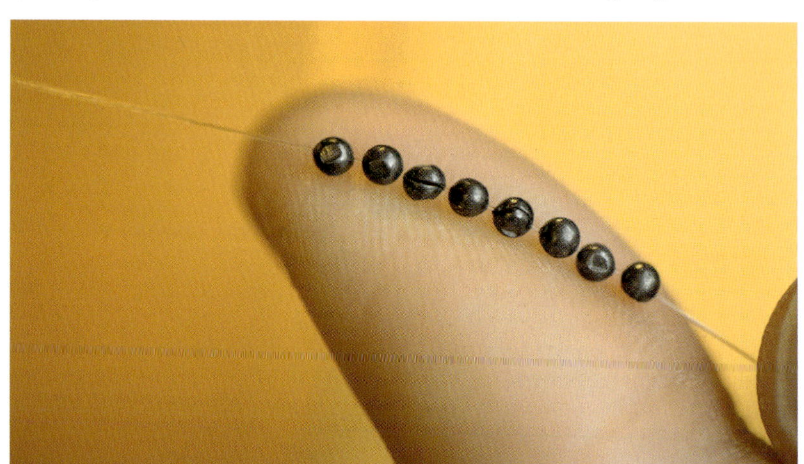

'carbon slim'. Basically it's a slim profile float, with a carbon, black glass or wire stem. My love affair with this pattern started with the iconic Preston Chianti, which has been around for 20 plus years and which I still use for light silverfish work in winter. The one downfall of the Chianti is the strength of the eye. It wasn't originally designed with carp fishing in mind, so I do step things up to a stronger pattern when it comes to bigger fish. This is where I move on to The RW Maggies - and I have these from 4x10 to 4x16 featuring everything from a 1.5mm diameter bristle to a 2mm bristle.

For bigger baits, or when targeting bigger fish I will happily use the thicker bristle, while the thinner bristle is kept for targeting finicky biting fish on tougher days. I use carbon stems for 90% of my fishing, but I do sometimes like the additional stability of a wire stem for expander pellets, or if there is a bit of a wind on the water.

The beauty of this slim profile is it's super sensitive, and also when used with a carbon stem follows your bait down as it falls through the water, so it's perfect for catching fish on the drop as well as on the deck.

On days when there is a wind on, or if I want more stability, or if fishing in deep water I choose what are usually referred to as 'Chimp' or 'Pinger' patterns. This is a rugby ball shaped body with a wire stem, and hollow plastic bristle. The real plus to this pattern is stability. It's great when fishing with big baits for big fish, you can even leave a bit of bristle out of the water so you can read what is happening if it suits.

For fishing on the bottom in shallow water, I will either use one of the small 'carbon slim' patterns, or a dumpy little float like the RW Muddie. These are always fished with the bulk down, the idea being to pin the bait to the bottom and keep it there until a fish sucks it in. For bigger baits and fishing down the margins, it's an RW Margin which does the same job.

Finally, my shallow floats. It's either a Jigga, an MW Cookie

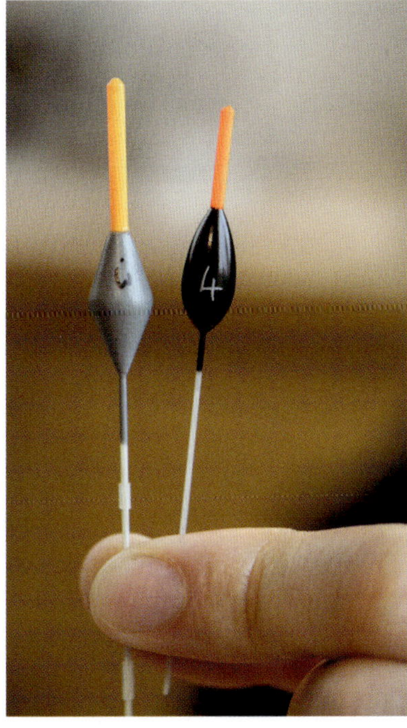

> **_These are personal choices, similar float patterns from other makers will generally work equally well if you prefer them._**

for long lining or mugging or an RW Shallow No1 or No2. The No1 (dibber) is used in depths less than a foot, the other up to two feet. If I'm fishing in depths greater than two feet, I will use one of the carbon slims.

As you can see, I don't use a million floats, eight patterns basically cover the whole spectrum for me, but I'm confident in the ones that I do use,

ABOVE:
A label writer makes it easy to identify everything on the bank.

LEFT:
The RW Muddies are used for nailing small baits to the bottom. For bigger baits down the edge, it's the Mick Wilkinson Margins.

RIGHT:
It's always worth paying a bit extra for pure PTFE bushes.

BELOW:
Note how I have the bad running in a loop, for maximum strength.

and know how they work and how to read them.

Hooks/ Hooklengths

I feel a bit guilty writing this next paragraph, as what I'm about to say would, a few years ago, have been seriously frowned upon. I never tie my own hooks.

The fact is, I can't do it anywhere near as quickly or as well as Dean Forster, a friend who I pay to do them for me. I'm simply not that dexterous, especially when it comes to tying ▶

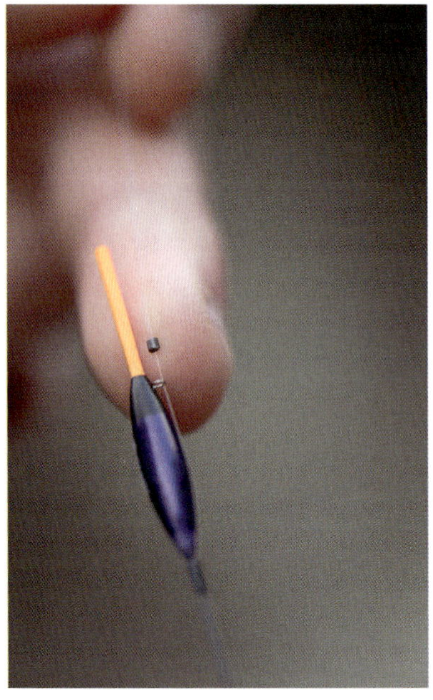

Carrying a range of different length hooklengths helps you adapt to how fish are feeding on the day.

> **"** *The one downfall of the Chianti is the strength of the eye. It wasn't originally designed with carp fishing in mind.* **"**

small hooks, and things like bands on light lines. To be properly covered for all commercial fishing these days, you need a fair few patterns and lengths tied up, too. If you are someone who maybe struggles for time, or if like me you're just a bit slow and cack handed, I would definitely recommend taking advantage of one of the professional hook tying services that are out there - using one has made me more prepared than I have ever been. Google 'hook

ABOVE LEFT: These Colmic Micro Cut weights are perfect for trimming or fine tuning the shotting on your rigs...

ABOVE RIGHT: ...and sneaking one behind the float eye means you can slide it up the line to give yourself more bristle if the float sits too low.

BELOW LEFT: The 'Andy Bennett' connection method is used on hollow elastics...

BELOW RIGHT: ... And the simple 'crow's foot' is favoured on lighter ones.

tying services' and you'll be amazed at the number of options.

So, what do I use and why? I'd say one hook pattern covers me for half of my fishing, and that is the Guru SLWG. This Teflon coated beauty is medium gauge, but super strong. Its round bend makes it perfect for pellets, meat, worms and positive fishing with maggots and casters.

I use these in the spade version for direct hooking, or the eyed version for banding/hair rigging. In terms of hooklength length and diameter I carry these in 12in, 8in, 6in, 4in, and 2in. For 90% of my fishing it's a six inch hooklength, the shorter ones only really coming into play when targeting shallow water.

> **"** *What I'm about to say would, a few years ago, have been seriously frowned upon. I never tie my own hooks.* **"**

The long ones are used for fishing over depth, on the waggler, or as spares - after all you can always shorten a longer hooklength to fill any gaps in your armoury that you may desperately need.

In terms of lighter patterns, I use the Guru F1 pellets for F1s, or heavy silverfish work. In the coldest weather, I'll scale down to a green Gamakatsu for light, small fish work.

For feeder fishing for carp, there are two key patterns - a Guru QM1 for big fish work, or a smaller Preston KKM for standard sized F1s and smaller carp. Again, I carry these tied up with bands and spikes to suit different hookbaits. Lengthwise, it's 4in, 5in, and 12in. For most of my silverfish work, I again favour the F1 pellet in a size 16. These are tied twelve inches long to 0.09mm Supplex fluorocarbon.

I've touched on hooklength material above. I love fluorocarbon for silverfish, so use this for all my natural fishing and commercial silverfish, but I do favour Preston's Reflo Power for targeting bigger fish - so this is my mainstay for commercial fishing rigs and hooklengths. ■

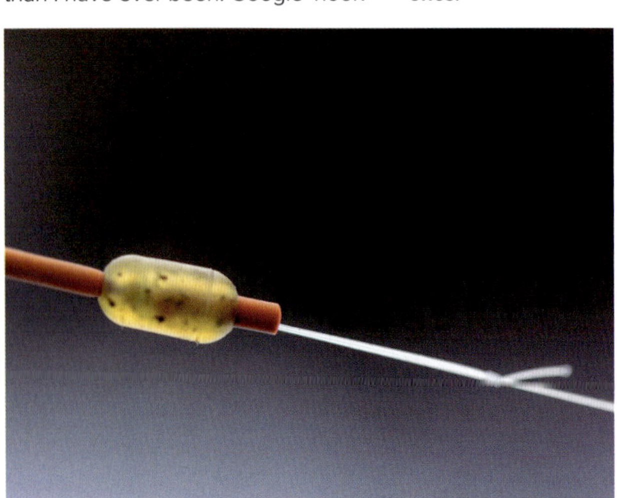

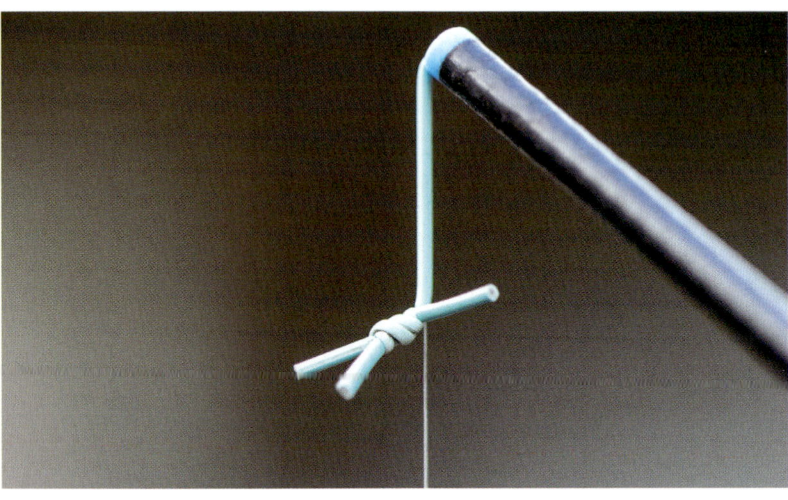

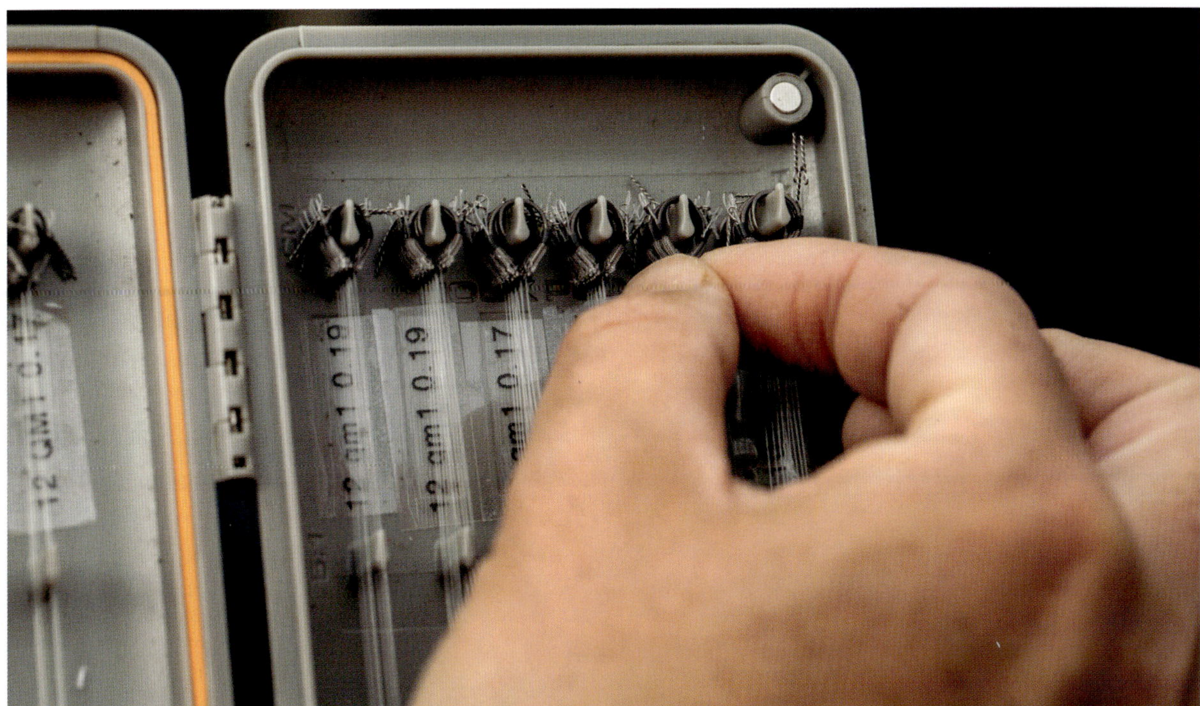

LEFT:
Guru QM1 hooks for bagging big carp on rod and line - but smaller Preston KKMs are used for lighter work.

BELOW:
Lost Treasure. We all have patterns of floats that work for us. When you find one - stock up, before it's discontinued, like my beloved Chianti.

INFLUENCER

When it comes to preparation, I've learned more from close friend Matt Godfrey than anyone. We lived together in a bachelor pad for four years down in Daventry when we worked on *Match Fishing* magazine, and I got to see the sheer dedication that he puts into his preparation. It wasn't so much the amount of prep that he did, but the attention to detail that most impressed me. If something wasn't perfect, he would simply discard it and start again. I saw him cut up and re-tie hundreds of rigs and hooks over the years just because he had found an improved pattern, or tweak. And that, I soon concluded, is the difference between professional thinking, and those that just make do.

USEFUL RESOURCES

Want to take your match fishing to the next level? Here are five resources you will quickly become addicted to.

Winning Ways!

The online home of Andy May and Jamie Hughes, *Winning Ways* was the brainchild of content creator, Richard Chapman. With multiple

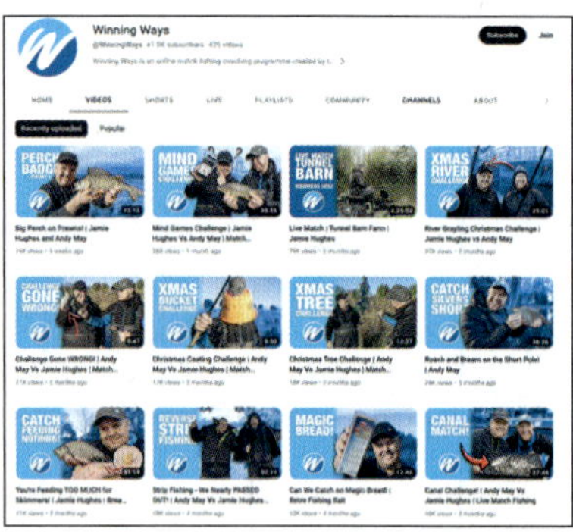

videos uploaded every week the channel covers everything from match blogs to fun challenges, live streams and live matches. For a small fee, you can pay to join the members area, where there is a host of content with other anglers, too.

Visit: https://www.youtube.com/c/WinningWays

Match Focus

As well as being one of the best commercial anglers in the country, Paul Holland is the model professional match angler, analysing every area of his game in a bid to

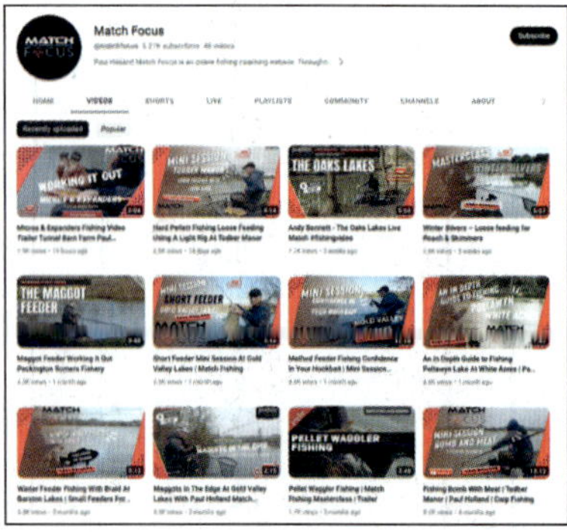

constantly improve. In his *Match Focus*, you will find instructional videos, match blogs, live streams, and live matches. He also features Andy Bennett as a regular guest, including him in live streams and live matches too.

Visit: https://www.matchfocus.co.uk/

Preston Innovations

With over 25 years at the top of the match fishing game, it's little surprise that Preston Innovations have one of the best libraries of video content out there! Star anglers like Des Shipp, Andy Power and Andy May make for a fascinating

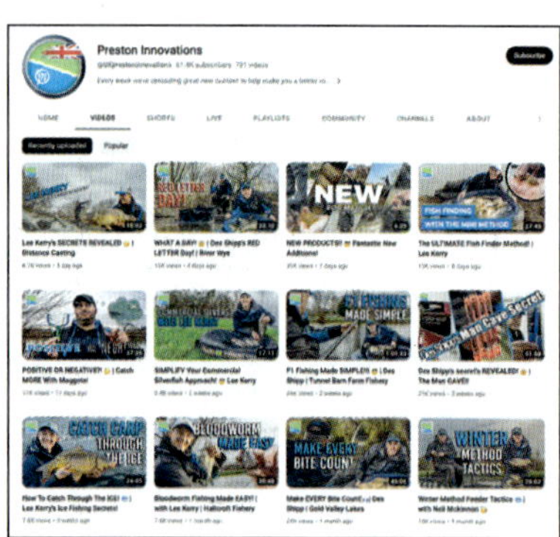

archive - covering just about every match fishing method you can think of! And the best thing? They are all completely free to view.

Visit: https://www.youtube.com/@UKprestoninnovations

Tackle Guru

These guys have taken match fishing media to the next level over the last few years, with state-of-the-art filming equipment, and some of the best anglers on the planet. Look out for their ground-breaking *'Underwater'* series, as well as

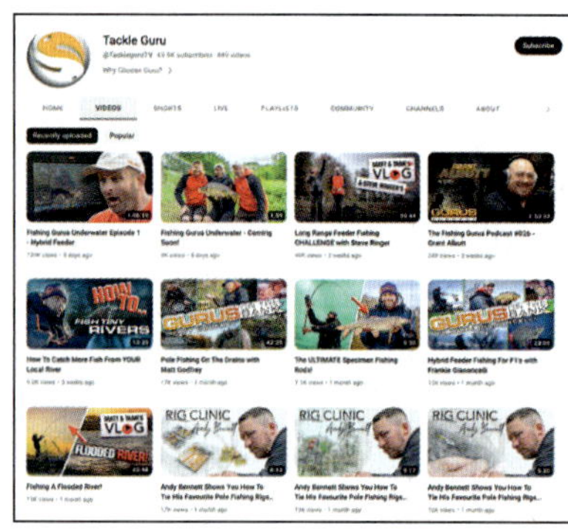

the much talked about *'Ringer Vs Bennett'* catalogue of head to heads. Again, totally free to view.

Visit: https://www.youtube.com/@TackleguruTV

Catch More Media

Founded by the author back in 2017, Catch More Media has built up one of the best catalogues of match fishing related video content on the internet. From event coverage to instructional pieces with star anglers, and of course the popular *'Review'* series of tackle reviews. Over 500 videos are free to view, plus there is the option of a paid platform for extra content.

Visit: https://www.youtube.com/@catchmoremedia

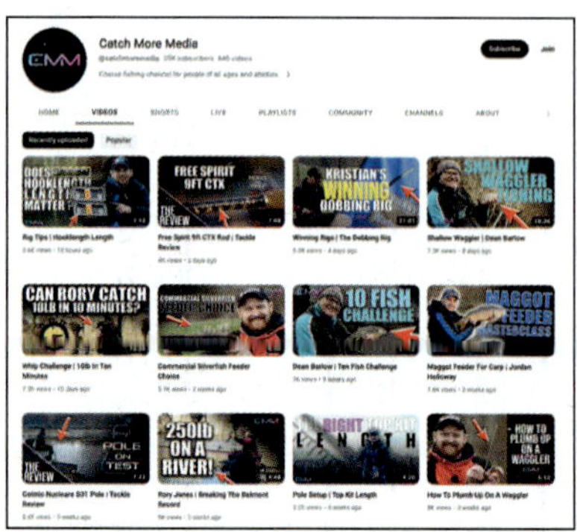